A GUIDE TO SPANISH FROM CHILE

LANGUAGE BABEL, INC.

Published by Language Babel, Inc., San Juan, Puerto Rico
Originally Published in July, 2010 by RIL Editores, Santiago de Chile

United States Edition ©2011. Version 1.0
Interior Design: Diana Caballero - diana@speakinglatino.com

For ordering information or special discounts for bulk purchases, please contact Language Babel, Inc. 1357 Ashford Ave., PMB 384, San Juan, PR 00907 or by e-mail to *info@speakinglatino.com.*

Jared Romey also publishes a blog and materials of other Spanish speaking countries. For more information about Speaking Latino, visit our web site at *www.SpeakingLatino.com.*

Printed in the United States of America by Language Babel, Inc.

ISBN-10: 0983840539 (paperback)
ISBN-13: 978-0-9838405-3-4
Printed in the United States of America by Language Babel, Inc.

Other books in the Speaking Latino Series:

- Speaking Boricua
- Speaking Phrases Boricua
- Speaking Argento

Other books by Language Babel:

- Baby Names from Puerto Rico
- Nombres de bebés de Puerto Rico

Table of Contents

ENGLISH

ESPAÑOL

QUICK VOCABULARY GUIDES

But that's the glory of foreign travel, as far as I am concerned. I don't want to know what people are talking about. I can't think of anything that excites a greater sense of childlike wonder than to be in a country where you are ignorant of almost everything. Suddenly you are five years old again. You can't read anything, you have only the most rudimentary sense of how things work, you can't even reliably cross a street without endangering your life. Your whole existence becomes a series of interesting guesses.

–Bill Bryson
Neither Here nor There: Travels in Europe

Travel is fatal to prejudice, bigotry and narrow-mindedness and many of our people need it sorely on those accounts. Broad, wholesome, charitable views of men and things cannot be acquired by vegetating in one little corner of the earth all one's lifetime.

–Mark Twain
Innocents Abroad

Introduction

It's been almost 12 years since I first arrived in Chile. At the time my Spanish was semi-functional, slow and, according to my then recently-acquired Chilean colleagues, somewhat Mexican (NOTE: Yesterday I was informed it's apparently now Central American!). Since then I have lived in two other Spanish speaking countries, lost the Mexican accent and am often more comfortable speaking Spanish than English. My Spanish, at this point, is a hodgepodge of vocabulary, pronunciation and grammar pulled from several countries, which may only be described as, well, a hodgepodge.

I still remember that one of the strangest things for me to accept during my learning process had to do with why the hell I'd spent years in classes, and yet a large portion of the words I'd learned didn't do me a damn bit of good in Chile. At the time it annoyed me more than anything, but since then I've learned to enjoy those differences, and have, in fact, spent a significant part of my time learning about them. It still amazes me that depending on where you are *chiringa*, *barrilete*, *papalote*, *cometa* or *volantín* all mean the same thing. Or that *bicho* in some places can turn a fast food employee blush-red, while in others it's a mere bug (my sincere apologies to the young lady).

Surprisingly, this has turned into a long-term project for me, with four books soon to be available, as well as learning aids and a website. My hope is to help people communicate more easily and to have fun during the learning process.

Chile is an amazing place where I can walk off the plane and in five minutes feel at home. I have some of the best friends in the world here. Santiago is an entertaining place to visit, to relax and to socialize. For me, it is always a wonderful escape.

Jared

Santiago
January 27th, 2009

Acknowledgements

Without a doubt, it would have been impossible for me to publish this book had I not had the help of Jessica Liberona. She spent countless hours with me expanding, explaining and understanding the material found in this book. Rosa Ester Zuñiga also proved to be of vital importance, especially in the late stages. In addition, Daniel Felipe Muñoz, Pilar Morán and Paula Parra helped me along the way. Thank you to all five for spending their precious little free time to teach me something of their language.

Anyone who knows Claudia Bravo will not be surprised to hear that she contributed vastly to the *garabatos* throughout the book. It is a sincere compliment to say that she has the mouth of a salty old sailor and has provided me endless laughs throughout our friendship.

Thanks to Diana Caballero who helped me at the end to make this book more concise.

Mercedes López Tarnassi (mmlopeztarnassi@gmail.com) translated the beginning sections into Spanish wonderfully.

I must also include an expression of gratitude to John Brennan and Alvaro Taboada, the authors of an amazing book called *How to Survive in The Chilean Jungle*. Their book not only helped me along during my first months in Chile, it also guided me into publishing my first book for Puerto Rico.

This book actually began, unbeknownst to anyone, including myself, in July 1997 when I arrived in Chile. From my first few hours here when my pizza was served with an egg on top (silly me thought that *huevo* was a euphemism for some typical pizza ingredient... who the hell puts egg on their pizza!) to my current visit learning about *tribus urbanas*, *ponciar* and the *dieta del gringo*, *Speaking Chileno* has been a collaborative effort. Everyone that pushed, prodded and poked me along into understanding Chileno should take some of the credit. To each of you, my gratitude.

How to Use this Guide

Before starting, it is important to highlight that this is not an academic, all-inclusive dictionary. Nor is there any scientific basis for what appears here. This is a guide based on my personal experience and research. There will be, without a doubt, disagreement with something I have written here. If you have the time, write me and share your comments or correct me. My personal experiences are based on extensive "exposure" to Chilean, Argentine and Puerto Rican Spanish, as well as contact with several other countries' Spanish, and because of this my views will be slanted to comparisons among those three countries.

There are a couple general ideas to keep in mind as you peruse the book. For example, the words are written as close to their grammatically correct spellings as possible. This is not always easy or clear, given that the same word may be pronounced several ways, may drop some letters in the pronunciation, and may in some cases have entered into the daily verbal lexicon only recently, not having yet allowed sufficient time for a general spelling to be accepted. The pronunciation section will help you track down the exact location of some of these words.

Also, with the influence of text messages and computer shorthand, many of the spellings you may see in the real world (or the Internet world) aren't the correct ones. For instance, *huevón* may appear as *weón*. My best advice for you in trying to figure out how *weón* is written would be to say it out loud (but, please, in a soft voice and not directed at anyone... to avoid a random street altercation), apply whatever basic Spanish rules you know, and look it up. Barring that, ask someone for help.

You will see the following symbols throughout the book, which are meant to make your life easier:

Symbols

★ Common word - the most common words you will run into.

💣 Dangerous word - these are either insulting to someone or just flat out naughty words.

[$] Money - words related to money or finance.

Since this is a guide to Chilean slang, I have left out many of the more common definitions for words. For example *muerte* does not include the definition "death". It only includes the colloquial usage in Chile.

When a word appears with "o/a" as in *desubicado/a* this refers to the need to apply the masculine (*desubicado*) or the feminine case (*desubicada*), depending on the sex of the word used.

Speak Like a Chilean

Why, you ask, would you want to speak exactly like a Chilean? A few reasons come to mind. The most important and perhaps obvious is to communicate better. Ask a Chilean how much it will cost you to take *una guagua* to Pucón, and it's more than slightly possible you may have to explain yourself to the police after being arrested. In Puerto Rico, for example this word means "bus", but in Chile it would be "baby".

There's also the challenge involved in learning a culture enough to mimic it, or at least to fit in. It feels quite good when your Spanish is fluent enough that someone doesn't recognize where you're from, or that you're not a native speaker.

Perhaps the best reason is to make people laugh. It's always entertaining to hear a foreigner use typical slang phrases, words and pronunciation. Just try walking up to your Chilean friends and say *"Chucha la Hueá"* (pronounced *choo-cha la way-ah*). You're gonna get a laugh from someone, if only because they're not used to a foreigner talking like that.

How do you achieve this? Focus on the basics. There are four major components to speaking like a Chilean. They are:

1. Vocabulary
2. Grammar
3. Pronunciation
4. Intonation

Vocabulary is perhaps the most time consuming. However, by using Speaking Chileno's vocabulary insets, by learning common Chilean words (marked with the symbol ★) and by listening to conversations and pulling out common phrases, you should quickly be practicing your Chilean vocabulary.

Grammar. Yuck!! Actually, it's not that bad because with only a couple simple guidelines your grammar *a la Chile* will be easy to speak. The Grammar section that follows will help (I said it's easy... see, the section's only 2 pages long).

Again, with Pronunciation, there's really not a lot to cover. Follow the few simple guidelines that appear in this section and you'll be accused of having a Chilean accent in no time.

In my opinion, the hardest of the four areas is to mimic the Intonation of a language consistently. This requires lots and lots of practice (at least for me). What I want to do here is to make you aware of some of the typical Chilean nuances, so you have a base from which you may continue exploring.

Chileans, more so than most other Spanish speaking people, have a pronounced rhythm to their sentences, and this rhythm can change the meaning of a sentence. For example, the phrase *muy malo* can take on different meanings depending on how it is pronounced. To say *muy malo* (pronounced *mwe ma-lo*), with short, concise syllables means "very bad" as in a bad person or bad behavior. On the other hand, to pronounce it *mweee maaaaaaAAAlo* dragging out the As and using a higher voice as you progress through the As is more likely to mean something of bad quality.

Generally speaking, Chileans vary the pitch of their words and phrases more so than I have heard in other countries. This is especially applicable to vowel sounds. For consonants such as C or CH the sound is short and hard and pronounced (more aspirated than other Spanish speakers, to use the technical term). Another observation is that the typical Chilean voice seems to me to be a higher pitch than that from other Spanish countries.

As a last hint, phone conversations are always fun to listen to. In short clips of time, you hear conversations rich in slang, local pronunciations and intonations. Just don't get caught eavesdropping!

Grammar

Here are a few samples of Chilean deviations from common Spanish grammar, based on my experiences. As always, I would love to receive any other contributions you may run across.

1. **en la mañana/tarde/noche**
   The widespread use of these phrases in Chile, beginning with the preposition *en,* led me to believe that this is the correct phrase for "in the morning/afternoon/evening". I found out several years later only after moving away from Chile that the grammatically correct preposition is *por* as in *por la tarde*. You will probably only ever hear *en…* in Chile.

2. **re-**
   The prefix re- for any word demonstrates "extra" of whatever is said. For example, *re-cansado* would mean really or extremely tired. The sentence *La Claudia tiene un vestido re-fashion* would mean that *Claudia has an extremely fashionable dress.*

3. **subir para arriba**
   Since *subir para arriba* means "to go up upstairs" it is redundant and therefore grammatically incorrect. Similar phrases are *salir para afuera* (to leave for outside), *entrar para adentro* (to enter inside), and *bajar para abajo* (to go down downstairs) are common yet, since they are redundant, are grammatically incorrect. The correct structure would be either *ir arriba* as in *voy arriba* or *subir* as in *él sube.*

4. **cachai, entendí**
   Here's the short version of this one (on advice of the Boredom Police I deleted the more technical description). Most of the time in Chile (and most other Spanish speaking countries) verbs that end in AR are conjugated using *-as* for the second person singular TU (for instance *tú cachas*), and *-er* and *-ir* verbs are with *-es* (for example *tú entiendes* or *tú sientes*). In Chile, you will often hear an *-ai* or *-i* ending (as in *cachai, entendi* or *senti*). This is extremely informal and most often used among friends.

Example:
René, anda a comprarme un chaleco. ¿Me entendi?... René, ¿me cachai, o no?

Translation: René, head out to buy me a sweater. Got it?... René, you get me or not?

5. **-ito**

The suffix *-ito* is extremely common in spoken Chilean and has at least three different uses:

The first use is to understate something, as in the difference between the *café está cargado* or the *café está cargadito.* Normally *cargadito* would mean that the coffee is a little strong, less strong than *cargado*, but here it actually means that the coffee is really strong, even stronger than *cargado.*

It can also signify a small amount or portion of something. For instance, *dame una cucharadita de los porotos granados*, would mean give me a little bit, as in a small portion of the *porotos granados.*

Third, it communicates affection. As an example, *vente mi chanchito y te doy la papa*, would be a typical phrase used with your son. You aren't really saying that your kid's a little pig. The translation is *Come here my little piglet and I'll give you your (milk) bottle.*

6. **Soy**

Normally, the word *soy* is the first person conjugation for the verb *ser* and means *I am*. However, in some instances in spoken Chilean it will mean *you*. For example, the phrase *¡Soy porfiado!* means that <u>you are</u> *porfiado* instead of what it should mean which is <u>*I am*</u> *porfiado*. The best way to pick up on this is to decide if the person is pissed at you for something or not, and from there figure out what they meant.

Pronunciation

Again, I only want to point at a couple examples of Chilean pronunciation, to start you on your way as you begin to notice the nuances of the spoken Spanish in Chile. Please keep in mind that pronunciation hints in this section are based on English sounds (with probably a slight American slant).

1. **CH as an English SH sound**
   Some Chileans pronounce all words with *ch* (including Chile) as if it were an English *sh* sound (*shi-lé* to mean Chile).

2. **Words ending in a vowel and then *-do* or *-da* lose the letter D**
   Words such as *tendido*, *patada*, *amasado*, and *patudo* will most often sound like *tendío, patá, amasao* or *patúo* where the speaker will drop the D completely. The AO sound is pronounced like OU in *ouch* or OW in *cow*. In the case of *-ada* ending words like *patada*, one of the vowels is completely eliminated. The result is *patá* with the accent replacing the missing vowel (be sure to understand the difference in pronunciation between *pata* and *patá*, as these are different words).

3. **Phrase "*para el*" or "*para la*" is shortened**
   The phrase *para el* becomes *pa'l* to create only one word (pronounced like PAL in *palm*). In the case of *para la* it remains two words but loses a syllable, to result in *pá la*. For example, the phrase *quedar para la cagada* becomes *quedar pá la cagá* (rule 2 above).

4. **A word ending in the letter A immediately followed by another word beginning in the letter D, drops the D**
   The common phrase *a donde la viste* becomes *a 'onde la viste*, dropping the D. As another example, *cabeza de pescado* is pronounced as *cabeza 'e pescao.*

5. **Words ending in *-von* drop the V**
   The *-vón* ending in a word, as in the prevalent word *huevón*, drops the V and is pronounced *hue-ón* (way-un).

6. **Errors in pronunciation**

As in with all languages, you may run across people that mispronounce a word, making it even harder for you to understand the sentence. These common mispronunciations will help you look out for other similar mistakes as you learn Chilean.

Keptchup to say ketchup
Picza or pipza for pizza
Rempujar for empujar
Resfalar for resbalar
Toballa for toalla
Ampoa or ampoha for ampolla

Gestures

Speaking like a local is not the whole answer to fitting in. Any culture has mannerisms and gestures that mark you as someone from around the corner, or someone from another world.

Many of these gestures are so natural for locals (I am avoiding using the word natives, as non-native people often pick up the local gestures after being in the new culture for a short time), that most people will not realize that they are using gestures not understood by foreigners.

Here are a few of those gestures that you will no doubt run into (and perhaps copy!) after spending a few days in Chile.

1. **Handshake, hug, 3 back-pats and another handshake**
   This one is obligatory and is probably the first you will learn if you're a guy. When one male greets another male friend (often after not seeing each other for a few weeks or months) the first step is a quick handshake, immediately followed into a hug (one arm below the other guy's armpit, and the other arm over his shoulder), three pats on the back using both hands, release the hug, and another quick handshake.

   BONUS: To really go native, throw in the phrase *¿Cómo estai po hueón?* as you initiate the first handshake.

2. **One hand cupped and covering an eye**
   This is a possible response when asked if your blind date, or another person, is attractive or not. It basically means the person in question was REALLY ugly, annoying, a bad catch, or all of the above.

   This gesture also means that you screwed something up or that things didn't go well, for instance on an exam at school.

3. **One hand straight up and down, touching your forehead in the middle a time or two (as in an axe splitting your head in half)**
   This means that you have a hangover. The action is similar to an axe hitting your forehead, as in a splitting headache!

4. **One hand making a V using the thumb and index finger, like forming a gun with your hand, and then raising it to your mouth (index/gun finger pointing left or right)**
Used to communicate that someone is full of crap, that he is basically making up a story or is lying. It also means that the person is a constant liar or is always stretching the truth.

Introducción

Hace casi 12 años hice mi primer viaje a Chile. En esa época, mi español era semi-funcional, lento y según mis compañeros chilenos a quienes recién estaba conociendo, sonaba un poco mexicano. (Aclaración: ayer me informaron que ahora mi acento suena, aparentemente, centroamericano). Desde entonces, viví en otros dos países de habla hispana, se me fue el acento mexicano y a veces me siento más cómodo hablando español que inglés. Mi español en este momento es una mezcolanza de vocabulario, pronunciación y gramática adquiridos en varios países y que sólo puede definirse como eso, una mezcolanza.

Todavía recuerdo que una de las cosas más absurdas de aceptar durante mi proceso de aprendizaje era por qué demonios, habiendo tomado clases durante tantos años, gran parte de las palabras que había aprendido no me servían ni un poquito en Chile. En el momento, más que nada me molestaba, pero desde entonces aprendí a disfrutar de esas diferencias, y de hecho, he dedicado gran parte de mi tiempo a aprenderlas. Todavía me sorprende pensar que según la ubicación geográfica, las palabras *chiringa, barrilete, papalote, cometa* y *volantín* signifiquen lo mismo. O que la palabra *bicho* en algunas partes haga sonrojar a la empleada del local de comida rápida mientras que en otros, sea literalmente un simple insecto (mis sinceras disculpas a la señorita del restaurante).

De manera inesperada, esto se convirtió en un proyecto a largo plazo. Pronto habrá cuatro libros publicados, junto con material didáctico y un sitio Web. Lo que espero es poder ayudar a que la gente se comunique de manera más fácil y que se divierta durante el proceso de aprendizaje.

Chile es un lugar increíble, donde puedo bajarme del avión y a los cinco minutos sentirme que estoy en casa. Aquí tengo algunos de mis mejores amigos del mundo. Santiago es un lugar entretenido para visitar, relajarse y conocer gente. Para mí, siempre es un lugar maravilloso para una escapada.

Jared

Santiago
27 de enero de 2009

Agradecimientos

Sin lugar a duda, hubiera sido imposible publicar este trabajo sin la ayuda de Jessica Liberona. Pasamos incontables horas juntos expandiendo, explicando y comprendiendo el material de este libro. Rosa Ester Zuñiga también resultó imprescindible, en especial en las etapas finales. Además, me ayudó la participación de Daniel Felipe Muñoz, Pilar Morán y Paula Parra en el desarrollo del libro. A ellos cinco les agradezco haber invertido su valioso y escaso tiempo libre en enseñarme detalles sobre su idioma.

Cualquiera que conozca a Claudia Bravo no se sorprendería si le contara lo importante que fue su aporte con los garabatos incluidos en el libro. Es una malhablada y lo digo como un sincero halago ya que durante nuestra amistad me ha hecho reír sin parar.

Gracias a Diana Caballero que me ayudó en la etapa final a que este libro fuera más conciso.

Mercedes López Tarnassi (mmlopeztarnassi@gmail.com) tradujo al español las secciones de introducción en forma excelente.

También debo expresar mi gratitud hacia John Brennan y Álvaro Taboada, los autores de un libro maravilloso titulado *How to Survive in The Chilean Jungle*. Su libro no sólo me ayudó durante mis primeros meses en Chile sino que también me sirvió de guía para publicar mi primera obra para Puerto Rico.

En realidad, este libro comenzó sin que nadie lo supiera, ni yo mismo, en julio de 1997 cuando recién llegaba a Chile. Desde mis primeras horas aquí cuando me sirvieron la pizza que había encargado con un huevo encima (¡qué tonto! Pensaba que *huevo* era un eufemismo para algún ingrediente típico de pizza... ¡a quién se le ocurre ponerle un huevo encima!), hasta mi visita actual, donde aprendí sobre las *tribus urbanas*, el significado de *ponciar* y *la dieta del gringo*, *Speaking Chileno* ha sido un esfuerzo de cooperación. Todos los que me impulsaron, me animaron y me alentaron en mi proceso de comprensión del chileno deben atribuirse parte del crédito. A cada uno de ustedes, mi agradecimiento.

Cómo Usar Esta Guía

Antes de comenzar, es importante destacar que este libro no es un diccionario académico ni abarca la totalidad. Tampoco hay ningún tipo de sustento científico del contenido del mismo. Se trata de una guía en base a mis vivencias personales y mi trabajo de investigación. Sin duda, habrá quienes no estén de acuerdo con algo de lo que escribí y de ser así, si tienen tiempo, los invito a que me escriban y compartan sus observaciones o me corrijan. Mi experiencia personal se basa en una amplia "exposición" al español chileno, argentino y puertorriqueño, entre otros países de habla hispana, y por eso me inclino a expresar mis opiniones comparando estos tres países.

Deben tener en cuenta una serie de reglas generales en la lectura de este libro. Por ejemplo, las palabras están escritas lo más aproximadamente posible a su forma gramatical correcta. La ortografía no es siempre tan fácil y clara, dado que la misma palabra puede pronunciarse de diferentes maneras, o a veces hay letras que se escriben pero no se pronuncian, o en algunos casos, son palabras incorporadas recientemente al léxico cotidiano y no ha pasado el tiempo suficiente para plasmar su ortografía general. La sección de pronunciación ayuda al lector a rastrear la ubicación exacta de estas palabras.

Además, con la influencia de las abreviaturas utilizadas en los mensajes de texto y la comunicación informática, muchas de las formas de escribir una palabra que vemos en el mundo real (o en el mundo de Internet) no son las correctas. Por ejemplo, *huevón*, puede aparecer escrita como *weón*. Mi mejor consejo para que puedan darse una idea de cómo escribir *weón* es decirla en voz alta (pero no a viva voz ni dirigiéndose a nadie… para evitar cualquier tipo de pelea callejera), aplicar las reglas básicas de español que conozcan y luego buscarla en algún diccionario. Más allá de eso, la otra opción es pedirle ayuda a alguien.

A lo largo del libro, verán los siguientes símbolos cuyo propósito es hacerles la vida más fácil:

Símbolos

★ Palabras comunes - las palabras más frecuentes con las que van a encontrarse

💣 Palabras peligrosas - son insultos o malas palabras, groserías o términos ofensivos

[$] Dinero - estas palabras están relacionadas con el dinero y las finanzas

Como esta es una guía de jerga chilena, dejé afuera muchas de las definiciones más comunes de las palabras. Por ejemplo, *muerte* no incluye la definición propia de la palabra. Sólo incluye la explicación de su uso coloquial en Chile.

Cuando una palabra aparece con "o/a" como por ejemplo, *desubicado/a*, se refiere a la necesidad de aplicar la forma masculina (*desubicado*) o femenina (*desubicada*) de acuerdo con el género de la palabra utilizada.

Hablar Como Un Chileno

Se preguntarán porqué querrían hablar exactamente como un chileno. Se me ocurren algunos motivos. El más importante y quizás más obvio es para comunicarse mejor. Pregúntenle a un chileno cuánto les costará tomarse una *guagua* a Pucón; es muy probable que tengan que dar largas explicaciones a la policía después de haber sido arrestados. En Puerto Rico, por ejemplo, esta palabra significa "micro" o "bus" mientras que en Chile quiere decir "bebé".

Otro de los desafíos es aprender la cultura de tal manera de poder mimetizarse o al menos integrarse. Es agradable la sensación de hablar español de manera tan fluida que los demás no reconozcan de dónde eres o no se den cuenta de que no es tu lengua materna.

Quizás el mejor de los motivos es hacer reír a la gente. Es divertido escuchar a un extranjero utilizar frases, palabras y pronunciaciones típicas de la jerga local. Prueben acercándose a sus amigos chilenos y diciéndoles "Chucha la Hueá". Se van a reír sólo porque no les resulta habitual que un extranjero hable de esa forma.

Ahora bien, ¿cómo se logra? Concéntrense en lo esencial. Hay cuatro elementos principales a tener en cuenta para hablar como un chileno y son:

1. Vocabulario
2. Gramática
3. Pronunciación
4. Entonación

El vocabulario es quizás la parte que más tiempo lleva. Sin embargo, podrán hablar chileno enseguida utilizando los recuadros de vocabulario de *Speaking Chileno*, aprendiendo palabras comunes del chileno (marcadas con el símbolo ★) y aprovechando las conversaciones para extraer frases de uso común.

Gramática. ¡Puaj! En realidad, no es tan terrible ya que con sólo un par de pautas sencillas, les va a resultar fácil poner en práctica la gramática a la Chile. La siguiente sección de gramática (en la página 23) los ayudará (les dije que era fácil… la sección sólo tiene 2 páginas).

Les reitero que en la sección de pronunciación no hay demasiado para cubrir. Si siguen las simples pautas que aparecen en esta sección, se los acusará de tener un acento chileno en menos de lo que canta un gallo.

A mi parecer, la más difícil de las cuatro áreas es la de imitar la entonación de un idioma de manera sistemática. Esto requiere muchísima práctica (por lo menos para mí). Mi intención en esta sección es ponerlos al tanto de algunos de los matices típicos del español chileno para brindarles una base a partir de la que podrán seguir explorando.

Los chilenos, más que la mayoría del resto de los hispanohablantes, tienen un ritmo pronunciado en el hablar, y este ritmo puede cambiar el significado de las oraciones. Por ejemplo, la frase *muy malo* puede tener dos significados diferentes depende de cómo sea pronunciada. Decir *muy malo*, con sílabas cortas y concisas significa literalmente que algo es malo, como ser una mala persona o una mala conducta. Por otro lado, si se pronuncia *muyyy maaaaaaAAAlo* arrastrando las A y en un tono más alto, a medida que se estiran las A, es más probable que haga referencia a algo de mala calidad.

En general, los chilenos varían el tono de las palabras y las frases más que en otros países. Esto se aplica especialmente a las vocales. Para las consonantes C y CH, el sonido es corto, fuerte y pronunciado (más aspiradas, para utilizar el término técnico). Otra observación es que a mí me dio la impresión de que la voz típica de un chileno es más aguda que la de otros hispanohablantes.

Como última pauta, las conversaciones telefónicas siempre proporcionan un momento de diversión. En un rato nomás, pueden escuchar conversaciones muy ricas en modismos, pronunciación y entonación locales. ¡Pero que no los pesquen escuchando a escondidas!

Gramática

Estos son algunos ejemplos de desviaciones de la gramática convencional, en base a mi experiencia. Como les dije anteriormente, me encantaría recibir todos los aportes que se les ocurran compartir conmigo.

1. **en la mañana/tarde/noche**
   El uso generalizado de estas frases encabezadas por la preposición *en* me llevaron a pensar que ésta era la preposición correcta. Varios años más tarde y habiéndome ido de Chile descubrí que la preposición gramaticalmente correcta era *por* como en la frase *por la tarde*. Probablemente sólo escuche *en...* en Chile.

2. **re-**
   El prefijo *re-* ante cualquier palabra se utiliza para darle una connotación más extrema. Por ejemplo, *re-cansado* significa muy cansado o sumamente cansado. En la oración *La Claudia tiene un vestido re-fashion* significa que *Claudia tiene un vestido sumamente de moda.*

3. **subir para arriba**
   La frase *subir para arriba* es una redundancia y por lo tanto, es gramaticalmente incorrecta. Lo mismo sucede con las frases *salir para afuera, entrar para adentro* y *bajar para abajo* que si bien son de uso común, gramaticalmente son incorrectas. La estructura correcta sería *ir arriba* (voy arriba) o *subir* (subo).

4. **cachai, entendí**
   Ésta es la versión abreviada de su uso (según los consejos del Control de Aburrimiento suprimí las descripciones más técnicas). Casi siempre, tanto en Chile como en el resto de los países de habla hispana, los verbos terminados en AR se conjugan con la terminación *-as* para la segunda persona del singular Tú (por ejemplo, *tú cachas*) y los verbos terminados en ER e IR se conjugan con la terminación -es (por ejemplo, *tú entiendes* o *tú sientes*). En Chile, con frecuencia se escuchan las terminaciones *–ai* o *-i* (como en *cachai*, *entendí* o *sentí*). Esto es sumamente informal y en general se utiliza entre amigos.

Ejemplo:
Chileno: *René, anda a comprarme un chaleco. ¿Me entendi?... René, ¿me cachai, o no?*

Español neutro: René, anda a comprarme un chaleco. ¿Me entiendes?... René, ¿te queda claro, no?

5. **-ito**

   El sufijo *-ito* es sumamente común en el lenguaje oral y tiene por lo menos tres usos diferentes:

   Se utiliza para dar un valor diminutivo a algo. Observemos las frases *el café está cargado* y *el café está cargadito.* Literalmente, *cargadito* quiere decir que el café está un poco fuerte, pero de acuerdo con el uso en este contexto significa que el café está muy fuerte, más fuerte que *cargado.*

   También quiere decir una pequeña cantidad o porción de algo. Por ejemplo, *dame una cucharadita de los porotos granados* quiere decir dame un poquito, una pequeña porción de porotos granados.

   Tercero, es una muestra verbal de cariño. Por ejemplo, *vente mi chanchito y te doy la papa*, es una frase típica de una madre hacia un hijo. No quiere decir que el hijo sea un pequeño chancho/puerco/cerdo.

6. **Soy**

   En general, la palabra *soy* es la conjugación de la primera persona del singular del verbo *ser.* Sin embargo, en algunos casos en el lenguaje oral significa tú. Por ejemplo, la frase *¡Soy porfiado!* significa *¡Eres porfiado!* en lugar de hacer referencia al sujeto que lo dice. Para captarlo, la mejor técnica es determinar primero si la persona que lo dice está enojada por algún motivo, y a partir de ahí, entender qué quiso decir.

Pronunciación

Sólo quiero señalar algunos ejemplos de la pronunciación chilena para darles una orientación inicial en el proceso de identificar los matices del español hablado en Chile. Tengan en cuenta que las pautas de pronunciación en esta sección se basan en sonidos del inglés (probablemente con una leve inclinación norteamericana).

1. **CH como el sonido SH del inglés**

   Algunos chilenos pronuncian todas las palabras con *ch* (inclusive Chile) como si fuera el sonido *sh* en inglés (*shi-lé* = Chile).

2. **Las palabras terminadas en vocal seguida de -do o -da pierden la letra D**

   Las palabras tales como *tendido, patada, amasado* y *patudo* por lo general suenan *tendío, patá, amasao* o *patúo*, donde el orador omite la D por completo. El sonido AO se pronuncia parecida a AU en *aula*. En el caso de las palabras terminadas en *-ada* en palabras como *patada*, una de las vocales se elimina por completo. El resultado es *patá*, donde el acento reemplaza a la consonante omitida (asegúrense de entender la diferencia entre *pata* y *patá* ya que son palabras diferentes.)

3. **La frase "para el" o "para la" se corta**

   La frase *para el* se transforma en *p'al* y pasa a formar una sola palabra (que se pronuncia PAL como palma). En el caso de *para la*, se conservan las dos palabras pero se transforma en *pá la*. Por ejemplo, la frase *quedar para la cagada* se transforma en *quedar pá la cagá* (ver regla 2 más arriba).

4. **La letra D se elimina cuando una palabra terminada en A está seguida de otra que comienza con D**

   La frase de uso frecuente *a donde* la viste se convierte en *a 'onde* la viste al eliminarse la D. Otro ejemplo es la frase cabeza de pescado que se pronuncia *cabeza 'e pescao*.

5. **Se elimina la letra V en las palabras terminadas en –von**

   La terminación *-vón*, como en la palabra de uso corriente *huevón*, se pronuncia sin la V de modo que se transforma en *hue-ón*.

6. **Errores en pronunciación**

Como en todos los idiomas, es normal encontrarse con gente que pronuncie mal ciertas palabras, y esto hace más difícil comprender una oración. Estos errores en pronunciación los ayudarán a estar atentos a la presencia de otros parecidos en la medida en que aprenden chileno.

Keptchup por *ketchup*
Picza o *pipza* por *pizza*
Rempujar por *empujar*
Resfalar por *resbalar*
Toballa por *toalla*
Ampoa o *ampoha* por *ampolla*

Gestos

Hablar como local no es lo único que se necesita para integrarse. Todas las culturas tienen gestos que determinan si alguien es de la zona o si viene de otra parte del mundo.

Muchos de estos gestos son tan naturales para los locales (evito utilizar la palabra nativos porque en general los no nativos también adquieren los gestos locales al poco tiempo de compartir una nueva cultura) que la mayoría ni se da cuenta de que están utilizando gestos que los extranjeros no entienden.

Estos son algunos de los gestos con los que sin duda se van a encontrar (¡y quizás copiar!) después de unos pocos días en Chile.

1. **Apretón de manos, abrazo, tres palmadas en la espalda y otro apretón de manos**

   Este gesto es esencial y probablemente el primero que los hombres van a aprender. Cuando dos amigos varones se saludan (en general si hace unas semanas o meses que no se ven) se dan un fugaz apretón de manos, seguido inmediatamente de un abrazo (un brazo por debajo de la axila del compañero, y el otro, por encima del hombro), tres palmadas en la espalda utilizando las dos manos, sueltan el abrazo y se dan otro apretón de manos.

   EXTRA: para quedar realmente como un nativo, metan la frase *¿Cómo estai po hueón?* al comienzo del primer apretón de manos.

2. **La mano ahuecada tapando un ojo**

   Esta es una respuesta posible si alguien nos pregunta si nuestra cita a ciegas u otra persona es atractiva. Básicamente, significa que la persona en cuestión es REALMENTE fea, molesta y un mal partido.

   Otro significado es meter la pata con algo o que las cosas no salieron bien, por ejemplo, reprobar un examen.

3. **La mano estirada, golpeando el medio de la frente una o dos veces (como si fuera un hacha partiéndote la cabeza a la mitad)**
   Esto significa que tienes resaca. El gesto es como un hacha dándole un golpe a la frente, ¡un dolor de cabeza que te la parte al medio!

4. **Los dedos pulgar e índice en V, como si fueran una pistola, cerca de la boca (con el índice apuntando hacia la izquierda o hacia la derecha)**
   Se utiliza para comunicar que algo es pura mentira, que alguien está inventando una historia o está mintiendo. También significa que alguien es un mentiroso empedernido o que siempre distorsiona la verdad.

SPEAKING CHILENO

A Guide to Spanish from Chile

LEXICON:

A

a cagar: to the end, all out, all the way.

a cagar no más: damn the consequences.

a calzón quitado: no holds barred, holding nothing back, straight to the point. *Hablemos entonces* ***a calzón quitado.***

a cheliar: go out drinking (beer). *Anoche salí* ***a cheliar*** *con mis amigas.*

a chupar: go out drinking. *Vamos* ***a chupar*** *mucho porque es el primer día de vacaciones.*

a colación: have lunch. *Vamos* ***a colación****, tengo hambre.*

a concho: all out, completely, all the way. *Hay que vivir* ***a concho****, disfrutar de todo; nunca se sabe cuando se acaba la vida.*

• a calzón quitado •

¿a dónde la viste?

★ **¿a dónde la viste?:** are you nuts?, no way, I don't believe you, you're way off. *Escuché por ahí que te van a ofrecer otro puesto mucho mejor.* ***¿A dónde la viste?***

a la americana: 1) a pot luck meal, where each person takes something to eat. *Mi cumpleaños va a ser* ***a la americana****, estoy sin ni uno.* 2) going Dutch, each person pays their own portion. *Vamos al cine* ***a la americana*** *el sábado.*

a la coche guagua: freeloader. *Me carga, este siempre anda* ***a la coche guagua.***

a la fe: without resources, without a possibility that something occurs, just believing in God.

a la hora del pico: damn late. *Con la Ange siempre llegamos* ***a la hora del pico*** *a todas partes.*

a la hora que se me pare el culo / hoyo / poto: whenever the hell I want. *Estoy de vacaciones, me levanto* ***a la hora que se me pare el hoyo.***

a la paraguaya: sex standing up. *Me encanta* ***a la paraguaya.***

a la pinta: something well done. *Me gustó el traje, me quedó* ***a la pinta.***

a la vuelta de la rueda: really slowly. *Sorry, llegué tarde porque la micro se vino* ***a la vuelta de la rueda.***

a lapa: piggyback.

• a lapa •

a lo comando: all out, with full energy.

a mango: all out, all the way, full speed ahead.

a medio filo: a bit drunk, buzzed. *Tomé un poco y quedé **a medio filo.***

a mil: all out, all the way, full steam ahead.

a morir: until the end.

a palos con el águila: broke, penniless.

a pata: on foot, without transportation. *Mi gimnasio me queda 15 minutos **a pata.***

a pata pelada: barefoot. *A mi hijo le encanta andar **a pata pelá.***

a patada con las piedras: broke, penniless.

a patada con los piojos: broke, no money. *La plata no me alcanza para salir, ando **a patás con los piojos**.*

a poto pelado: 1) naked 2) by the seat of your pants, without planning or preparation. *No tengo toda la información, así que voy a exponer así no más, **a poto pelado.***

a poto suelto: sound asleep, completely out. *Cuando esté de vacaciones voy a dormir **a poto suelto**.*

a prueba de tontos: easy, idiot proof. *El examen estuvo **a prueba de tontos**.*

a sangre de pato: not worried about pain/risk.

a toda raja: amazing, awesome. *La fiesta fue fantástica, **a toda raja**.*

a todo cachete: something cool, awesome, fun, the best, all you could possibly want.

a todo chancho: full blast, maximum volume, all out, all the way. *Me encanta escuchar música y cantar **a todo chancho.***

• a todo chancho •

a todo ritmo: all out, all the way. *El carrete fue **a todo ritmo**, lo pasamos súper bien.*

a trasmano: out of the way.

abeja maya: an effeminate man. *Saravia siempre está hablando como **abeja maya**.*

abrazar para atrás: a name for gays, means "hugging behind".

abrirse: get out of here, leave, move on.

abuelaless: granny style women's underwear. *En los días R debo usar* ***abuelaless.***

abutagado/a: completely stuffed, gorged from food. *Comí tanto que estoy* ***abutagado.***

💣 **acabar:** to have an orgasm.

acabronarse: to keep the best for oneself. *Se sentó en la mejor mesa y se* ***acabronó*** *con los tragos.*

acartonado: not natural. *Se veía mal de traje, muy* ***acartonado.***

acaso: perhaps, by the way.

achacado: depressed, sad. *Se sacó mala nota y anda todo* ***achacao.***

achacarse: to get worked up about, pissed off about.

achaplinarse: to stand up, to bail on, to cancel at the last moment. *Apuesto que Daniel va a* ***achaplinarse*** *otra vez, siempre lo hace.*

achoclonar: to be squished together, generally in reference to too many people in a tight place. *En mi familia somos bien* ***achoclonados.***

achuncharse: to freeze up, during a presentation, conversation, or an important event.

achuntar: 1) to hit the nail on the head, to guess correctly, dead on. ***Achuntaste*** *el precio exacto del auto.* 2) to successfully insert something into another thing, for example a key into the door lock. *Estoy muy ebrio, no le voy a* ***achuntar*** *a la chapa.*

aclararse: to be able to solve something by yourself.

aconcharse los meados: actually means to NOT be able to piss because you're so scared, but the translation would be to piss yourself from fright. *Ayer casi me asaltan, y se me* ***aconcharon los meaos.***

afilar: 1) to have sex. 2) to scold someone.

afinar la paila: to try to listen to, listen up. *Ya poh,* ***afina la paila****, no estás entendiendo nada.*

aforrar: to beat, hit.

[$] **AFP:** stands for *Administradora de Fondo de Pensiones* and refers to any of numerous private pension fund companies.

agachar el moño: when you know that you did something wrong and have to assume the consequences. *Me mandé un condoro, obligado a* ***agachar el moño*** *si me retan.*

agarrado: in love with, perhaps to the point of being blind about the other person, extremely wrapped up with someone. *Javier está súper* ***agarrado*** *y la mina es pesá.*

agarrar: to make out with, suck face, do everything but have sex.

agarrar hasta los fierros calientes: to blindly trust or believe in. *Es más tonto,* ***agarra hasta los fierros calientes.***

agarrar papa: to believe everything blindly.

★ **agarrar para el hueveo:** 1) to tease someone, to jerk their chain. *Me equivoqué en una sola palabra y me* ***agarraron pa'l hueveo*** *toda la noche.* 2) to not take a romantic relationship seriously, a fling, just mess around with. *El desgraciado solo me* ***agarró pa'l hueveo****, mientras la polola estaba de viaje.*

★ **agarrar para el leseo:** 1) to tease someone, to jerk their chain. *Me equivoqué en una sola palabra y me* ***agarraron pa'l leseo*** *toda la noche.* 2) to not take a romantic relationship seriously, a fling, just mess around with. *El desgraciado sólo me* ***agarró pa'l leseo****, mientras la polola estaba de viaje.*

agarrar para la palanca: to tease someone. *Con lo que le pasó lo vamos a* ***agarrar para la palanca*** *todo el día.*

agarrar vuelo: to get going, to jumpstart, to take off (figuratively). *El negocio partió lento pero está comenzando a* ***agarrar vuelo.***

agarrararse del moño: to argue, fight. *En la fiesta de anoche las minas se* ***agarraron del moño.***

agilado: fool.

💣 **agua de caña:** a faggot.

aguachar: to dominate someone, to put him in a submissive position. *Y el perro* *dejó de ladrarle y se* ***agua-chó*** *a su lado.*

aguaitar: "looking at" but in a special way like waiting for something.

agüaite: to wait.

aguántame un cacho: wait a minute!! or Hold on! if you are on the phone. ***Aguántame un cachito*** *que voy al baño.*

[$] **aguinaldo:** an extra salary payment that companies make to employees for Chile's independence celebrations (*Fiestas Patrias*) or for Christmas.

agüita: hot water with herbs, orange or lemon peel, an after dinner tea used to settle the stomach.

agüita perra: an herbal tea after eating to help with digestion. *Me tomaría una* ***agüita perra*** *después de almuerzo.*

aguja: 1) insistent about some idea. *La Ange es súper* ***aguja****, molesta hasta que consigue lo que quiere.* 2) a womanizer, a guy that chases all the tail he can.

agujonear: to push or bug someone, for example, to finish something you requested.

ahí quedaste: 1) to get lost. 2) to be negatively surprised about a situation or some bad news.

ahuasado: a dense, dumb, shy person.

ahuevonado: dumb, stupid, idiotic, so stupid that what is obvious to everyone else, he/she doesn't realize. *Él es tan* ***ahuevonado*** *que no se da cuenta que le cobran de más por su teléfono.*

ají: 1) a hot pepper. 2) typical sauce made with ketchup or tomatoes and hot peppers, similar to Tabasco sauce.

ají en el poto: literally "hot peppers in the rear-end", something annoying or bothersome.

ajuerino: a foreigner, someone from "ajuera".

al agua: not valid, worthless. *Ese boleto de lotería es antiguo ya se fue* ***al agua.***

al choque: willing to fight.

al cuete: not well done, careless. *Como estaba apurado para salir, hice el aseo* ***al cuete.***

al gratin: for free. *La fiesta de despedida de Roberto fue todo* ***al gratin****.*

al hilo: right away, in a row, one after the other.

al hueso: straight to the point. *Ya dime, tengo prisa, vamos* ***al hueso.***

al lote: a bunch of stuff strewn around or unorganized. *La ropa de mi closet está* ***al lote.***

al ojo del amo engorda el caballo: things only work when the boss is watching over.

al otro litro: all set, finished. *Ya está todo bien, estamos* ***al otro litro.***

al pelo: to have sex without using protection.

al peo: same as *al cuete. Arreglé las maletas* ***al peo,*** *para irme rápido.*

al pil pil: a form of preparing seafood, potatoes or vegetables with a sauce made of garlic, butter and oil.

al seco: literally "to dry", bottom's up, in reference to finishing an alcoholic drink in one sip.

al tajo y con ajo: talk too much about something you shouldn't, or get angry with no reason.

al tirante: right away, immediately.

★ **al tiro:** right away, immediately. *Vamos a salir* ***al tiro,*** *solo tengo que ponerme los zapatos.*

• al tiro •

al toque: right away, immediately. *Partimos* ***al toque,*** *no esperemos más.*

al tres y al cuatro: bad off economically. *No puedo ir de vacaciones, ando* ***al tres y al cuatro.***

★ **alaraco:** someone that complains a lot about minor things, makes it sound worse than is really the case, a whiner. For example, someone with a small cold that thinks they are going to die. *Juan es* *muy **alaraco**; tuvo un pequeño resfrio y se quedó con licencia de una semana.*

💣 **alboadictos:** extreme fans of the Colo Colo soccer team.

albornoz: And you?, what about you?

alejada de la mano de Dios: a nice way of saying someone is ugly, literally "far from the hand of God".

aletazo: to beat someone with the fist. *Si no dejas de molestar te voy a dar un **aletazo**.*

aliado: a ham and cheese sandwich.

almacenes por ahí: refers to any place where stolen goods may be purchased.

💣 **almeja:** pussy.

almorrana: another term for hemorrhoids.

alpargata: means that something is very little or nothing compared to another thing. *Eso es una **alpargata** al lado de lo que hay que estudiar en la universidad.*

💣 **alpinista:** insulting term that uses a play on words of the word *pico*, which means a mountain peak, but also means dick. An *alpinista* is a woman that goes from peak to peak (alpinist) or dick to dick easily.

altirante: right away, right now.

alumbrado: someone that shows off the designer brands they have/use.

aluzaplaz: plastic wrap.

amacharse: to be manly, to man up, to grow some balls.

amarillo: a gay person still in the closet.

amarrete: someone who never shares (money, food, anything), stingy.

amerme: short for *amermelado.*

amermelado: goofball, dummy, doofus. ***¡Amermelao!*** *Te olvidaste dónde estacionaste el auto.*

amigay: term used for a masculine looking guy but that's really gay.

amigo/a con cover: a friend with "privileges" or with "benefits".

amigo/a con derechos (de raspe): a friend with "privileges" or with "benefits".

amigo/a con raspe: a friend with "privileges" or with "benefits".

amigo/a con ventajas: a friend with "privileges" or with "benefits".

amigui: a snobby word for friend.

amo: cool, someone who is the best in doing something.

amononarse: to get all dressed up. *Hay que **amononarse** para ir al casino, no podemos ir sport.*

amoroso: cute, nice, loving, caring. *Eduardo es muy **amoroso** con su familia.*

amotinado: when someone takes advantage of a particular situation to get everything for himself.

ampolleta: light bulb, another Spanish word is *bombilla.*

amurrarse: to get angry, not talk because of anger. *Como no le dieron permiso para ir a la fiesta se **amurró**.*

💣 **analfabestia:** completely stupid, ignorant.

anclar: literally "to anchor", used to refer to putting one foot on the ground to keep the room from spinning when you are drunk. *Llegué tan borracho que me tuve que **anclar** para poder dormir.*

anda a acostarte: expression used to say to someone that you don't agree with him/her.

💣 **andar a cagarse:** to tell someone to fuck off.

andar a cantarle a tu abuela: when someone is invited to leave a place because he/she is lying or talking stupid things. *Estaba borracho y decía tanta lesera que lo mandaron **a cantarle a tu abuela.***

anda a echarte sapolio: Leave!, Scram!, Beat it!

anda a echarte tanax: Get the hell outa here!, Beat it!

anda a freír monos al África: Get the hell outa here!

anda a huevear a los pacos: to tell someone to go bother someone else, literally "go screw with the pigs (as in cops)".

anda a lavarte el hoyo

• anda a lavarte el hoyo •

anda a lavarte el hoyo: Leave!, Scram!, Beat it!

andar a lo gringo: going commando, to not wear underwear.

anda a ver si está lloviendo afuera: Split!, Scram!, Get outa here!

anda a ver si está lloviendo en la esquina: phrase used, often with kids, to tell them to go away and stop bothering.

andar acumulado: to not have had sex in a long time.

andar aguja: to be suspicious of.

[$] **andar al 3 y al 4:** 1) to have no money. *Hasta que no me paguen,* ***ando al 3 y al 4****.* 2) to be a bad student.

andar ancho: phrase to describe someone that's bumping into other people, generally from being drunk.

andar botella: to be alone.

andar cero aporte: to not have a clue.

• andar a lo gringo •

andar choreado: to be pissed off, worked up about something.

andar churrete: to have diarrhea. *Me cayó mal la comida y por eso **ando churrete.***

andar CMR: a wedgie, to have your underwear way up your ass, stands for *calzón metido en la raja. Estoy incómoda, **ando CMR**.*

andar cocido: to be drunk.

andar como huasca: to be drunk, trashed.

andar como nalga: to be drunk.

★ **andar con:** to be dating someone in the early stages of the relationship, not officially boyfriend/girlfriend, this would be previous to *pololear. Juan **anda con** Jessica desde hace tres semanas.*

andar con caña: to be hung over.

andar con Cecilia: to be thirsty.

andar con el agua cortada: to be cut off from sex by your partner, generally for screwing up somehow.

andar con el culo en las manos: to be scared witless.

• andar con el culo en las manos •

• andar con el dragón •

andar con el dragón: to have a hangover, noticeable because everyone can smell it on your breath.

andar con el hacha: to have a hangover.

andar con el hachazo: to have a bad hangover. *Tomé tanto anoche que voy a* ***andar con el hachazo*** *todo el día.*

andar con la caña: to be hung over.

andar con la chispa: to be happy, content.

andar con la mona: to be hung over. *Anoche salí, tomé mucho y esta mañana* ***ando con la mona.***

andar con la pierna: to be accompanied by your significant other, literally "to be with the leg".

andar con la raja partida: to have your ass hurt from sitting so much.

andar con la regla: literally means that a woman has her period, but when used in reference to men, means that he is acting like a neurotic, emotional woman.

• andar con el hacha•

andar con la ruler: to have your period (for women).

• andar con la pierna •

andar con las riendas colgando: a man who asks permission from his wife to go out with his friends is said to have the horse reigns (that his wife controls him by) still hanging on him.

andar con los días R: to have your period (for women).

andar con los monos: to be annoyed or pissed off.

andar con marea roja: to have your period (for women).

andar con olor a lirio: to have one foot in the grave, extremely ill.

andar con sed: literally means to be thirsty, but when used often asks specifically if someone would like an alcoholic drink. ***¿Andai con sed?*** *Sí, dame un fanschop.*

andar con un diente largo: extremely hungry, famished, literally "to have a long tooth".

• andar con un diente largo •

[$] **andar cortina:** to have no money, broke. *Mi hermano siempre **anda cortina**.*

andar crítico: to be broke.

andar cuneteado: to have your underwear up your ass.

andar de farra: to go out partying. *A Daniel y sus amigos les encanta* ***andar de farra.***

andar de maleta: to be in a bad mood.

andar denso: phrase used to tell someone that they are being grouchy.

andar dulce: to have money, generally from just receiving it (as in not because you are rich, but because you just received money).

andar en cleta: to ride a bike.

andar en dodge: to be on foot, without a car. *¡****Ando en dodge****, en dos patas, poh!*

andar en la pitilla: to not have much money.

andar en pelota: to be naked.

[$] **andar en pelotillehue:** 1) to be naked. *Estaba solo en su casa y como hacía calor le gustaba* ***andar en pelotillehue.*** 2) to be without money.

andar enfiestado: buzzed, happy. *Desde mi cumpleaños que* ***ando enfiestado.***

andar finito: ironic term to say that someone swears a lot, that the person speaks crudely.

💣 **andar ganosa:** to be horny for sex now, comes from *andar con ganas*.

💣 **andar goteando:** to be horny, ready to screw.

andar happy: to be buzzed from alcohol or drugs to the point of being happy or amorous.

💣 **andar húmeda:** to be horny, ready to screw.

andar más botada que mina fea: to be ignored by everyone, literally "to be more ignored than an ugly chick".

andar mas doblado que churro: to be extremely trashed, drunk.

andar para el gato: to feel sick. *Estoy con gripe y* ***ando para el gato.***

andar para la corneta: to feel sick, bad or sad.

andar para la zorra: to feel sick, bad or sad.

andar pasado a flores: to have one foot in the grave, about to kick the bucket.

andar pasado a razoco: to smell stinky.

andar pasado a rodilla: to be dirty and stinky from not bathing, comes from smelling like feet and ass, since the knee (*rodilla*) is halfway between the two.

andar pasado a sobaco: to be stinky, literally "to smell like armpit".

andar pasteliando: to be distracted. *Cuando maneja **anda** puro **pasteleando**.*

[$] **andar pato:** to be broke.

[$] **andar patricio:** to not have any money.

andar picado: to be worked up because you lost a game or bet, often looking for revenge.

andar pickle: to reek of alcohol, to be pretty drunk.

andar pinchando: to make out with.

andar prendido: to have a lot of energy or enthusiasm.

andar quemada: to have bad luck.

andar raja: to be drunk.

andar rajado: to go fast. *No podemos **andar rajados** por Tobalaba, es peligroso.*

[$] **andar salado:** to be broke.

andar sapiando: to be spying, trying to see something specific.

[$] **andar sin ni uno:** to be without a cent, broke. *No puedo ir con ustedes al cine, **ando sin ni uno**.*

andar suelto de cuerpo: to be relaxed, without worries. *Debiera estar preocupado por la prueba de mañana, pero **anda todo suelto de cuerpo** carreteando.*

andar vendiendo: to have your fly open.

andarla vendiendo: to be lying.

ándate a la punta del cerro: to go to hell, to screw off.

💣 **ándate a la chucha:** to go to hell, to fuck off, fuck you.

💣 **ándate a la cresta:** to go to hell, to fuck off, get the hell out of here.

💣 **ándate a la mierda:** fuck-off, fuck you.

aniñado: someone that shows he is brave even when it's not necessary.

anotarse un poroto: to accomplish something good at work or with another person. *Consiguió el préstamo para la empresa, se **anotó un poroto.***

anticucho: a shish-kebab, skewer.

antofapasta: goofy term used to refer to the town *Antofagasta.*

antojar: to have a desire to have something, for example, a pregnant woman that wants chocolate.

apagar el calefont: to be gay.

apagar la tele: to be completely passed out drunk.

apañar: to be there for someone in trouble, to help someone out. *Ahora que perdió su trabajo, lo tengo que **apañar**.*

apechugar: to assume the consequences of one's actions/ decisions. *Se quiso ir de la casa de sus padres y ahora tiene que **apechugar** solo.*

aperkinado: someone who is controlled by someone else.

apernado: a person that is so confident in his position/ job, often because he has connections higher up. *Está **apernado** como director de la escuela.*

aperrado: brave, valiant, committed.

aperrar: all out, full, all the way.

apiernado: accompanied by your significant other.

apiñado: in a group, accompanied, not alone. *Nunca anda solo, siempre apiñado.*

★ **apitutado:** to use one's contacts to obtain something (a job) even though one is not necessarily qualified, well connected. *Ximena está **apitutada** en la pega porque es amiga del gerente.*

aplanador de calle: someone with no direction, no purpose. *Cacho que el hermano de ella es un **aplanador de calle.***

aplicar pausa: calm down, take it easy.

apollerado: uses a woman (mother or girlfriend) to hide from problems instead of facing them. *Lo dejé porque es un **apollerado**.*

aponchado/a: to be beyond someone's ability or means. *Yo nunca había manejado gente antes, y estoy **aponchada** con este cargo.*

aporrearse: to go all out to achieve something.

apotingado/a: to sit so comfortably that there is no way he/she will move. *Es tan flojo que llega a mi casa y se queda **apotingado** viendo TV.*

apotope: to be naked.

aprecue: to run away, comes from a combination of the two words *apretar cueva*.

apretar cachete: to run away, escape.

apretar cueva: to escape, get outa town, get away. *Llegaron los pacos y salieron **apretando cueva.***

💣 **apretar el asterisco:** to be worried, scared about something.

💣 **apretar el chico:** to be worried, scared about something.

apurar la causa: to do something quickly, speed up the pace. *Me queda poco tiempo para la presentación y no termino aún, tengo que **apurar la causa.***

★ **aquí estamos:** common response to someone asking you how you are or what's happening, means same old - same old, nothing new, literally "here we are", depending on what follows it can also mean so-so, not so hot. *¿Cómo estás? **Aquí estamos**, más o menos.*

aquí y en la quebrada del ají: it's the same everywhere.

💣 **araña peluda:** the hairy spider, in reference to pussy.

arrepotingarse: slide over, make room for the next person, etc. *Llegó la Monse así que **arrepotíngate** y cabemos todas en el sillón.*

arranado: with no energy, or desire to do anything. *Como la polola lo pateó, ahora pasa **arranado** en su casa.*

arrancarse los enanos para el bosque: to be crazy, mad, nuts. *Si lo escucharas hablar, te darías cuenta de que se le **arrancan los enanos para el bosque**.*

arrastrar el poncho: to be depressed, sad. *Anda **arras-***

trando el poncho *porque no le dieron permiso para viajar.*

arrastrar la bolsa del pan: points out the difference in someone's age, how they've grown up. *¡Mira mi vecina! ¡Como ha crecido!... ya no* ***arrastra la bolsa*** *del pan y cruza la calle sola.*

arrastrarse: to suck-up, kiss-ass.

arratonarse: to fight without all the energy, not give 100%, play defensively in sports. *El equipo siempre se* ***arratona*** *cuando juega contra Argentina.*

arreglado: wine served with fruit.

arreglar el cuerpo: to help recover from a hangover, literally "to fix the body" by eating, most often seafood.

arrejuntarse: to make up after a fight. *Mi hermano y su polola se* ***arrejuntaron****.*

arriba de la pelota: drunk, trashed or high.

arriba de la piñata: shit-faced drunk, trashed.

arriba del balón: drunk or high.

• arriba de la pelota •

arrollado primavera: term used for a Chinese spring roll.

arroz: someone that it is not important in a group, that does not contribute at all, a dead weight.

arroz quemado: to be gay. *A Ricky se le* ***quema el arroz.***

arrugar: to back out of, to chicken out, to give up.

arrugón: someone that makes a promise but doesn't follow through.

artista del cine: an annoying, egotistical person, that

thinks they're the shit. *Juan Pablo entró a la fiesta como **artista del cine**.*

asado: a barbecue (the party, not the actual grill).

aserruchar el piso: to try to screw someone over, without them noticing, to back stab.

así es la vida del pintor: that's just the way things are.

así no más: as is. *Ponte cualquier cosa, salgamos **así no más.***

asolapado: stupid without realizing it.

asopado: has no clue, lost, blind to the reality. *Ella siempre lo quiso, y el muy **asopado** nunca se dio cuenta.*

atacado: worried, concerned, nervous. *Jorge está **atacado** con los problemas del trabajo.*

★ **atado:** a problem, mess, or situation. *Estoy metida en un tremendo **atado** con mi ex.*

atadoso: someone that makes everything complicated, takes the easiest situation and makes it difficult, always has a problem with any situation.

atarantado: impulsive, without thinking of the consequences.

atinado: someone who's always right on the mark with the right opinion, the right solution, etc., the usage is always in a positive manner. *Me encanta su forma de ser, es siempre tan **atinado** para decir las cosas.*

atinar: 1) to make out. *La Ana se pasa soñando con **atinar** con Miguel.* 2) to guess correctly. *Tengo una habilidad especial para poder **atinar** con la talla del sostén de cualquier mina.* 3) to give something a try, for example a romantic relationship. *Ella tiene los ojos puestos en ti hace tiempo, ¿por qué no **atinas**?*

atontado: dazed, out of it, either from anesthesia or high on drugs. *El no decía nada coherente, estaba **atontado**.*

atorado: when you cannot wait to tell someone new gossip. *Estaba **atorada** por contar que estaba pololoeando.*

atornillar al revés: to do the things trying to prevent the group goal, working against the others. *Se nota que hay alguien acá que **atornilla al revés.***

atracar: to suck face with someone, heavy making out.

atrapado: a paranoid person who feels he is being observed or chased.

atraque: anything from making out to casual sex. *Ese tipo es el rey del* ***atraque****, no te metas con él.*

aturdido: dummy, slow, awkward, dorky. *Las piscolas que tomé anoche me dejaron medio* ***aturdida****.*

¡avíspate!: pay attention! *Por favor,* ***¡avíspate!****, necesito que hagas lo que te pedí.*

azul: a player or fan with the Universidad de Chile soccer team.

B

bacán: kick ass, cool, awesome, sweet.

bacilar: 1) to go out, hit the town, run around and have fun, live it up, to party. 2) to bug or bother someone.

bacilón: a great, wild time, often related to going out on the town, drinking, etc.

bailar con la coja: to always have bad luck, literally "to dance with the person that limps".

bailar con la fea: to have to do the difficult part of a task, literally "to dance with the ugly person".

bairón: the word for the son of a slutty woman who has sex with so many men that no one knows who the father is. *Nadie sabe quien es el papá del* ***bairón****.*

bajativo: an after dinner cordial to help the digestion, most often alcoholic, for example a *menta* or a *manzanilla* liqueur.

bajón: a drop in your level of happiness, enter into depression, lose faith.

bajón de porotos: diarrhea.

bakán: see *bacán*.

baldear la cubierta: to drink water before alcohol to keep from getting drunk.

baltiloca: term refers to the brand of beer Báltica, combines the name of the beer with the word *loca*, or crazy.

bandera roja: have your period.

barrer la plaza: to wipe your plate clean, especially using a piece of bread. *Cuando la comida me gusta, no dejo nada en el plato, siempre **barro la plaza**.*

barrida: when the police catch a group of people in just one operation, a sweep. *Entraron a ese bar e hicieron la tremenda **barrida**.*

barros jarpa: a ham and melted cheese sandwich.

barros luco: a beef and melted cheese sandwich.

barsa: shameless, fresh. *Este es súper **barsa**, me pidió plata prestada y no me la devuelve.*

barsudo: rude, act out of place, cross the line. *Oye no seai **barsuo** hueón devuelveme mi plata.*

bataclana: a slutty, low class, easy woman.

beatle: a turtleneck shirt.

★ **bencina:** gasoline.

besos y abrazos no sacan pedazos: advice sometimes given to another that means go out, have a good time, make out with the other person if you want, but don't get yourself into trouble (always in reference to sex).

bestia: term of endearment used with friends.

bicho raro: a weird individual, a strange bird.

bici: bicycle.

[$] **bicicleta:** financial concept when a person borrows money to pay previous debts and continues this indefinitely. *Vivo **bicicleteando** mis deudas.*

[$] **billete largo:** well-off, loaded.

[$] **billullo:** money, bucks, moola.

blanco y negro: nickname for the Colo Colo soccer team.

boca de chomba: a blabbermouth, blabs about the secrets of others. *El no sabía que ella era **boca de chomba**, y todos se enteraron del atraque.*

boca de tarro: a blabbermouth.

bodega: warehouse, other Spanish words are *almacén* or *depósito*.

bodrio: worthless, trashy in reference to a place or a person that doesn't contribute anything. *Nos fuimos apura-*

*dos del cine porque la película era un verdadero **bodrio**.*

[$] **boleta:** a basic receipt for purchases, which is different from a *factura*.

bolsear: when someone never pays for his things (drinks, food, etc.) and others have to pay for him. *Con la excusa de que está en la universidad siempre anda **bolseando** a sus amigos.*

bombero: a gas station attendant.

bombilla: drinking straw, other Spanish words are *pajita*, *sorbeto*, *popote*.

boni: short for *bonito/a*.

borgoña: drink of wine and fruit. *Me encanta el **borgoña** de durazno bien helado.*

bosta: a lazy, useless person.

botado: cheap, extremely inexpensive, a good bargain.

💣 **botar el diente de leche:** for a woman to lose her virginity.

botarse: to take something to the extreme, in a negative sense. *Desde que lo dejó la mujer, **se botó** al sexo y las drogas.*

botella de fanta: a fat woman with stomach rolls, just like a bottle of Fanta soda.

brígido: a difficult or complicated situation.

brillo: panorama, party, plans for the evening. *Hay un buen **brillo** esta noche.*

broca cochi: the inverse of *cabro chico*, or kid.

★ **bruja:** a term of endearment for a friend. *Oye, **bruja**, ¿por qué no me llamai mañana?*

buche: same as *barsudo*.

buena chuntería: good aim.

buena guacho: a greeting like "Hey dude".

💣 **buena naty:** a blow job.

★ **buena onda:** 1) a nice person, gives out good vibes. *Ese chico es **buena onda**.* 2) cool, sounds good.

buena perro: a greeting like "Hey dude".

buena tela: cool, good vibes, describes either a situation or a person.

★ **bueno/a para el hueveo:** this phrase has different meanings when used in reference to a man or a woman. When used to describe a man, it means that he loves to go out and drink, but in reference to a female, it means that she is slutty or easy.

bueno para el diente: someone with a healthy appetite, someone that enjoys eating.

bulla: fans of the Universidad de Chile soccer team.

buzo: sweatpants.

C

cabeza de agua: an airhead, someone with nothing but water in their head. *Siempre dicen que las rubias son* ***cabeza de agua***.

cabeza de pescado: stupid, foolish things that are said. *¡Para de hablar* ***cabezas de pescao*** *ajilao!*

cabeza de pollo: someone who almost always forgets things.

cabezón: smart, studious, geeky.

cabreado: boring.

cabritas: popcorn.

cabro: a kid. *Este* ***cabro*** *tiene que entender que no todo es así de fácil.*

★ **cabros chicos:** kids, slightly rude or insulting.

★ **cachar:** to understand, to get it.

cachilupi: cool, nice, good.

cachiporrearse: to show off what one has or owns. *No tiene en qué creerse, pero le encanta* ***cachiporrearse*** *de todo.*

cachito: 1) a hangnail. 2) a problem.

cacho: a mess, disaster, a problem that needs solving.

💣 **cacho de paragua:** someone with a penis that can't get hard, or is bent over.

cachurear: to sift through junk, antiques, old or thrown away items to look for something that may be useful.

cachureo: knick-knacks, stuff.

caerse al frasco: to drink too much for a long period of time. *No viene a trabajar más, parece que se* ***cayó al frasco.***

DRINKS / COPETE

These are all terms for drinks:

agüita: hot water with herbs, orange or lemon peel, an after dinner tea used to settle the stomach.

agüita perra: an herbal tea after eating to help with digestion.

arreglado: wine served with fruit.

bajativo: an after dinner cordial, to help the digestion, most often alcoholic, for example a *menta* or a *manzanilla* liqueur.

baltiloca: referes to the brand of beer Báltica, combines the name of the beer with the word *loca*, or crazy.

borgoña: drink of wine and fruit.

chela: a beer.

chicha: a sweet wine made from fermented fruit, most often made for special occasions such as *Fiestas Patrias*.

chimbombo: 1.25 gallon (5 liters) bottle of cheap punch, often of peach flavor.

cola de mono: an egg nog like Christmas drink.

cortado: an espresso coffee with a bit of milk.

doragua: insulting term used in reference to the brand of beer Dorada, combines the name of the beer with the word *agua*.

escupo: term that means spit, used to refer to the brand of beer Escudo, insulting the quality of the beer.

fanfaron: rum with orange Fanta.

fanschop: a draft beer mixed with orange flavored soda (generally Fanta).

golpeadito: a shot of liquor.

guarisnaque: any type of drink that you are not sure of the contents, for example an alcoholic beverage.

guatero: a bag of wine that comes inside boxed wine, always an extremely cheap wine.

jote: red wine with cola.

marcela: a beer.

menta: a mint-flavored after dinner cordial, used to help with the digestion.

DRINKS / COPETE, *continued*

mistela: a drink made with *aguardiente*, cinnamon, quince, orange peel and clove.

navegado: warm red wine prepared with sugar, spices (like cinnamon and cloves) and orange slices.

petaca: a liquor flask.

pichí de cangúro: white wine with pineapple juice, literally "kangaroo piss".

pichuncho: an alcoholic drink with *pisco* and martini liquor.

pipeño: an alcoholic drink similar to wine generally only made during Chile's independence celebrations (Fiestas Patrias).

piscola: a mix of *pisco* and a cola soda.

ponche: any type of wine punch with fruit added.

ronaldo: word to refer to rum, or *ron* in Spanish.

roncola: rum and coke, a combination of the words *ron* and *cola*.

schop: a draft beer.

submarino: beer with mint liquor.

terremoto: a drink made from white wine, ice cream and liquor.

tincola: term for red wine with cola.

tintolio: another term for red wine.

trago: a drink, a cocktail.

tropical: white wine with pineapple juice.

vaina: a drink made from wine, vermouth and egg.

vino navegado: heated red wine with sugar and orange rind, served hot.

whiscacho: a whiskey.

caerse el cassette: to share something that was supposed to be a secret.

café con piernas: these are small cafés, that generally only serve coffee, have standing room only (no tables) and the servers are always women in heels, and tight, extremely short skirts.

cafiche: someone that lives off his wife or girlfriend's work or efforts. *El novio de Elizabeth es un* ***cafiche****, no le ayuda con los gastos para ná.*

★ 💣 [$]: **cagado:** stingy, tight-fisted, especially in reference to money. *No salgo más contigo, eres muy* ***cagado****, no invitas ni una bebida.*

cagado de la cabeza: nuts, crazy, screwed in the head.

★ **cagado de la risa:** dying of laughter.

cagado del mate: nuts, crazy, screwed in the head.

★ 💣 **cagar:** 1) to take a shit. *Hace tres días que no* ***cago****, no sé que problema tengo.* 2) to be amazed, to die for. *Tienes que ver la nueva casa. Te* ***cagai****, tiene 15 piezas y 13 baños.* 3) to fuck over. *Cagué a Juan Pablo frente al jefe ayer.* 4) to be fucked up, really messed up. *Después del choque, los dos quedaron súper* ***cagados****.* 5) nuts, crazy, off your rocker. *¿Estai* ***cagado*** *de la cabeza, cómo puedes decir eso?* 6) screwed, messed up, over with. *El Luis tenía un asado pensado para hoy, pero después de la pelea con la pesada,* ***cagó*** *todo.*

💣 **cagarla:** to fuck up, screw up. *Trata de hacerlo bien, no vayas a* ***cagarla****.*

cagaste: you missed your chance. *No te puedo esperar más,* ***cagaste****.*

cahuín: 1) mix-ups, problems, sticky situations. 2) vindictive gossip.

cahuinear: to spread gossip, to create problems by gossiping.

cahuinero: someone that causes problems by running off at the mouth, or spreading gossip with the objective of causing problems. *La Marcela es más* ***cahuinera*** *que la chucha. Dejó la escoba con la Claudia.*

caído del catre: fool.

caldo de chancho: a person that no one wants to be around, disagreeable.

★ **calefont, calefón:** a water heater, most often run with natural gas.

💣 **calentar la sopa:** to be a cock-tease.

caleta: a lot of, a bunch of. *Después de ganar La Polla, Paula tiene* ***caleta*** *de plata.*

💣 **caliente:** 1) horny. 2) mad, annoyed, pissed off. 3) to have a strong need or desire of something. *Estoy* ***caliente*** *por comprar el nuevo Ipod.*

califa: flirtatious, horny, suggestive but to the point of making others uncomfortable. *Me molesta como me mira, es súper* ***califa***.

💣 **callaguaguas:** literally "baby quieters", in reference to a woman's breasts.

callampa: 1) mushrooms. 2) slums. *Hay comunas que aún tienen muchas* ***callampas***. 3) worthless.

callampear: to scold someone. *Si lo hago mal, seguro me van a* ***callampear***.

callulla: a huge nose. *Diego tiene una tremenda* ***callulla***.

calmado: relax, slow down a bit.

caluga: 1) a chewy, caramel-like candy. 2) a person that has a big nose. 3) a "sticky" person, someone who is always attached to you.

calugazo: a passionate kiss. *Él se acercó y delante de todos le dio el tremendo* ***calugazo***.

calzar: to commit someone to something, as in an appointment. *Me* ***calzaron*** *con ir a buscar a la abuela.*

calzones rotos: a fried dough pastry.

cambiarle el agua a las flores: to wash your rear end.

💣 **camboyana:** slut, whore.

caminar más que Kung Fu: to walk a whole lot. *Estoy raja, he* ***caminado más que Kung Fu.***

💣 **camino de tierra:** anal sex, literally "dirt path".

camote: annoying, someone that "sticks" to you, follows you around.

campeona de natación: insulting term to say that a woman has a flat chest and a flat ass, she is called a swimmer, or champion swimmer because of a play on words with swim (nada) and nothing (nada). *Nada por delante y nada por detrás* literally means swims front and back, but also means nothing in the front and nothing in the back. *La chica nueva es* ***campeona de natación****, la pobre.*

cana: jail.

★ **caña:** a hangover.

canapé: someone who wants to be in the middle of everything whether it be a party or a meeting.

★ **canchero:** a hip, happening person, outgoing, friendly, someone that people enjoy being around, someone with a pleasant personality. *Ese tipo es **re-canchero**, se maneja bien.*

cañones: rough, hard, noticeable hair, could be eyebrows, armpit, legs or wherever. *Debería ir a depilarme hoy, estoy llena de **cañones**.*

cantar Gardel: pay day. *Por fin es fin de mes, hoy **canta Gardel.***

💣 **canuto:** mildly insulting term for all non-catholic Christians. *Todos mis vecinos son **canutos**.*

★ **capaz que:** maybe, perhaps. ***Capaz que** mañana vaya al cine.*

capo: 1) the top expert, the most knowledgeable. *El chico es **capo** en esgrima.* 2) smart, keen astute. *Lo hace súper bien, es **capo**.*

captar: to understand.

cara de culo: a pissed off, annoyed, angry, sad or sickly expression. *¿Qué te pasa que andas con **cara de culo**?*

cara de nalga: shameless, someone that crosses the line.

cara de palo: point blank, not hold anything back, straight to the point, direct but to the point of being insulting, or to cross the line. *¡La muy **cara de palo** le dijo que no lo engañaba y él le creyó todo!*

cara de poto: literally "a butt face", refers to someone that has a depressed or sad look on their face.

cara de raja: 1) shameless, someone that crosses the line. 2) straight-out, pull no punches.

cara dura: shameless, beyond acceptable. *Es muy **cara dura** para venir a verme después de la cagada que dejó.*

★ **carabinero:** policeman, the name for the Chilean national police force. *Robaron mi auto, hay que llamar a **Carabineros**.*

caracho: a pissed off, annoyed or angry expression. *Otra vez está enojado, me puso el tremendo **caracho** cuando llegué.*

caracol: a type of shopping center that has a spiral walkway going up, with stores on the outside part of the walkway, similar to a snail's shape.

carapálida: a moon, as in two white butt-cheeks, not

BODY PARTS /PARTES DEL CUERPO

chacotero sentimental: a dick.

cola: rear end, heinie.

cuchara: another word for heart.

culo: ass.

guata: tummy.

paila: ear.

pata: foot.

pichula: a word for penis/ dick.

pico: a dick.

pirulín: a guy's wee-wee.

poto, potito: rear-end, heinie.

queque: rear-end.

tetas: tits.

toperoles: a woman's nipples.

traste: rear-end, bottom.

trompa: mouth.

tula: penis, when discussing with children.

zapallo: 1) big-headed 2) a big rear end.

the galaxy, light-the-night version.

carbonero: someone who likes to pit two people against each other, to create conflict.

★ **cargar:** to dislike. *Me **carga** ese tipo de música que escuchan los lolos.*

★ **carné:** the Chilean national identity card. *Se me perdió el **carné**.*

carne al disco: a type of BBQ that is cooked in a round disc. *Preparemos una **carne al disco** hoy en la noche.*

★ **carrete:** a night out on the town, out partying.

★ **carretear:** to go out on the town.

★ **carretero:** someone that continuously goes out to ***carretear.***

carretero a cagarse: a full out, extreme party animal.

★ **carta:** a restaurant menu, another Spanish word is *menú.*

[$] **cartola:** bank account statement.

cartonero: a person that goes through the street collecting cardboard from peoples' trash, for recycling.

cartucha: a person who shows a respectable image of herself, but she is really not at all respectable. *Se hace la **cartucha** pero sabe más que yo.*

cartucho/a: a square person, extremely conservative and reserved.

[$] **cash:** same as English. *No tengo **cash**, aquí ni se puede pagar con cheques o tarjeta.*

casino: a cafeteria, often at the workplace.

catete: mean-spirited, rude, annoying, bothersome.

cato: nickname for the Universidad Católica soccer team.

cazuela: a stew made from beef or chicken, potatoes, pumpkin and other vegetables, with a thin broth.

cebolla: romantic, emotional, comes from onions that make you cry.

cecina: a general term for any lunchmeat.

cero aporte: a useless, worthless person, that doesn't help out in any way.

chabacano: 1) not done properly, something that is finished but with little effort and not correctly. 2) tacky, in poor taste.

chacal: the best, tops, the max.

chacarero: a typical sandwich made of beef slices, tomato, green beans and green hot peppers, most often with *pan frica*. *Me encanta el **chacarero** que sirven acá.*

chacotear: to joke with, goof around with.

chacotero: a party animal. *Me cae bien, es súper **chacotero**.*

💣 **chacotero sentimental:** a dick.

chacra: a mess, a screw up. *En mi closet está la media **chacra**.*

chacreado: overdone, for example a song that is played so much on the radio everyone is tired of it.

chala: a sandal. *Se me cortó la huincha de la **chala** y no podía caminar.*

chalado: nuts.

chaleco: an open type of sweater, similar or the same as a cardigan.

chambreado: 1) buzzed, a bit drunk. 2) something slightly warm. *A mi me gusta tomar el vino **chambreado**.*

chambrear: 1) to warm wine to serve it, during winter especially. 2) buzzed, flush from alcohol.

💣 **champañazo:** a blowjob that finishes in her mouth.

chamullento: a liar, someone that talks a good game but is making it up.

chamullo: a lie.

chancaca: 1) a sweet sauce used on top of *sopaipillas*. 2) easy.

chancacazo: a strong blow. *Me pegué un tremendo **chancacazo** con la ventana, todavía me duele.*

chanchada: the act of betraying someone.

chanchito: a term of endearment for a child or partner.

chancho: 1) a belch. 2) a pig, used in reference to people, a disgusting person.

chancho en misa: out of place, out of sorts, disoriented.

chancho en piedra: a condiment prepared with chili peppers, onion, cilantro, garlic, tomato, salt, oil, and lemon, chopped up finely. *Qué top una carne a la parrilla y **chancho en piedra**, ¡me encanta!*

chanchullo: trap, deception.

chancletero/a: someone that only has daughters, but no sons.

chanfle: a banana kick in soccer, where the ball takes an extreme curve.

💣 **chano/a:** a sleazy, disgusting, gross person, trashy, low class. *Fui a un recital en Parque O'Higgins y estuvo lleno de **chanos**.*

chanta: a fake, false, a liar, cheater. *Es súper **chanta**, no hay que creerle nada.*

chantado: someone who stops drinking for a while.

★ **¡chao pescado!:** I'm outa here, see ya later alligator. ***Chao pescao**, me voy.*

chapa: fake name used for delinquents.

chaparrita: a hot dog with cheese wrapped in dough, like pigs in a blanket.

chaqueteo: speak badly about someone to others.

chaquetero: a wishy-washy person that changes their position on something depending on what's best for them at the moment.

★ **charcha:** 1) cheap, poorly made, worthless. 2) bad.

charchazo: a slap (in the face). *Si me sigue molestando, le voy a dar un buen **charchazo**.*

charchetas: the flab rolls hanging off a person's tummy.

charqui: beef jerky.

charquicán: a stew made from ground beef and different types of ground or finely chopped vegetables.

chasca: messed up hair, a rat's nest in your hair. *Me lavé el pelo y me quedó la tremenda **chasca**.*

chascarro: a funny, yet embarrassing situation.

chascón: a lot of hair, but messy.

chascona: unruly, tangled, messed up hair. *Mi sobrina siempre anda **chascona**.*

chato: a cool, nice or agreeable person.

chato/a: 1) worn out, dead tired. *He trabajado mucho, estoy **chata**.* 2) tired of, fed up with. (work, marriage, life). *Estoy **chato** con mi jefe, me tuvo trabajando todo el fin de semana.*

[$] **chaucha:** 1) pocket change, very little, a small amount. *Me costó una **chaucha** comprar el Ipod ya que era viejito ya.* 2) Run, here comes the fuzz!!!

chela: a beer.

chepa: a person who likes gossip. *Eli es súper **chepa**, siempre está pelando a alguien.*

chepear: to gossip.

chicha: a sweet wine made from fermented fruit, most often made for special occasions such as *Fiestas Patrias* in September. *En Fiestas Patrias Jared, Lily y yo tomamos **chicha** hasta quedar totalmente borrachos.*

chicha fresca: a constant flirt or tease.

chicotea los caracoles: get moving, let's go, come on we're late. *Vamos tarde, **chicotea los caracoles**.*

chilena(ita): a bicycle kick in soccer resulting in a goal.

chillón: a man who easily cries.

chimbombo: 1.25 gallon (5 liters) bottle of cheap punch, often of peach flavor.

[$] **chin chin:** pay in cash. *Si pago **chin chin** me hacen un buen descuento.*

chiquillo/a: 1) a child until about 12 years of age. 2) refers to one's close friends.

chiquiturris: little.

chirimoya: a fruit called sour sop in English, also known as *guanábana* in Spanish.

chirimoya alegre: a flavor often used in ice cream and yogurt that is a combination of *chirimoya* and orange.

chita la payasada: darn, shucks.

chiva: a lie. *Ya déjate, me has dicho solo **chivas**.*

chócale: word used when two people say the same thing at once, or when they coincide at something. *Yo también fui al estadio, **chócale**.*

chocarle: to bother, not get along with, not like. *Su actitud me **choca**, es un pesado.*

chocarse: to shock, to surprise.

chochos: curly hair.

chocleros: teeth.

choclo: corn, another Spanish word is *maíz*.

choclón: a crowd of people. *Había un tremendo **choclón** en la entrada del metro.*

chomba: sweater.

chori: cool, nice, good.

★ **choriado:** annoyed, completely fed-up with.

choripán: *chorizo* sausage and a piece of bread, often as an appetizer at barbecues.

💣 **choro:** 1) cute, nice, fun. *El vestido que la Sofía compró es bien **choro**.* 2) pussy.

chorrillana: a typical Chilean dish of french fries, beef, pork, chicken or sausage (or a mix of more than one) with scrambled eggs and fried onions.

chorrociento: a whole lot of, thousands of something. *Es muy caro viajar a Asia, son* ***chorrocientos*** *pesos.*

💣 **chucha:** 1) son of a bitch, shit. ***Chucha****, se me cayó el plato.* ***Chucha****, casi me caigo.* 2) pussy.

chuchunco city: Timbuktu, really far away.

★ **chueco:** 1) crooked, bent, twisted. *Mi cleta se quedó* ***chueca*** *después de la tremenda caída que tuve.* 2) someone that stood someone up, or doesn't follow through with a commitment, not reliable. *Es un* ***chueco****; le comenté algo en confianza, y se lo contó a su polola.*

chuecura: an unloyal act.

chuica: a big 5 liter (1.25 gallon) bottle used for wine or other drinks.

chuki: a bad person like the character Chucky in the horror movies.

chulo/a: sleazy, low class, trailer trash. *Es muy* ***chula****, no salgas con ella.*

chunchos: fans of the Universidad de Chile soccer team. *Me cargan los* ***chunchos****, porque soy garrero.*

chunchules: cow innards that are grilled and served at typical Chilean asados and parrilladas.

chunga: shucks, darn.

chupalla: a straw hat used by *huasos.*

chupamedias: a kiss up, a suck up. *Me cae mal, es súper* ***chupamedias*** *en la oficina.*

chupapata: kiss-up.

chupar: to drink alcohol excessively.

chupar las patas: kiss up to.

chupar más que orilla de playa: literally "to drink more than a beach's edge", refers to someone that drinks extensively but is not necessarily drunk.

chupe: a thick, creamy stew most often made with seafood.

chupete: a baby's pacifier.

chupete de fierro: a rude, mean, annoying person. *Me ha molestado mucho, es súper* ***chupete de fierro****, es muy camote.*

churrero: a hot guy.

churro: a hot guy.

chusca: an easy woman, a slut.

★ **chuta:** shucks, darn. *Ay **chuta**, me pegué en el dedo.*

cierre: zipper.

★ **¿cierto?:** right?, correct?, isn't that so?

💣 **cinco contra uno:** to jerk off, literally "five against one".

cintura de huevo: a fat person, literally "waist of an egg". *Estoy tan gorda que ya tengo **cintura de huevo**.*

cleta: a bike.

clínica: a private hospital, most often upscale with better facilities and care than in a *hospital* or *posta*.

COA: the special slang that prisoners use.

cochayuyo: a rust colored algae from the ocean, boiled and served in salads and stews.

★ **cochino:** 1) dirty. *Despúes de jugar todo el día afuera, Matías llegó tan **cochino** que lo tuvimos que bañar dos veces.* 2) dirty minded. *Luis siempre piensa **cochino**, tanto que no lo soporto.*

cocido: extremely drunk.

cocimiento: seafood, beef, sausage, pork, cooked in the ground, over coals and rocks that conduct the heat; typical from the Chiloé area of Chile.

💣 **cola:** 1) a line waiting for something. (for example, at the bank or at a cash register). 2) rear end, heinie. 3) a fag.

cola de mono: an egg nog like Christmas drink.

colación: lunch time at work or school. *El jefe no atiende a nadie en su hora de **colación**.*

colaless: G-string underwear, a thong.

colarse: 1) to butt in line. 2) to sneak in somewhere.

cole: a rubber band used by women to tie their hair back.

★ **colectivo:** a taxi that runs a fixed route and is shared with up to three other people.

colgar: to assault. *Ese lugar es súper peligroso, te pueden **colgar**.*

💣 **coliguacho:** a faggot, queer.

colleras: cuff links, other Spanish words are *gemelos* and *yuntas*.

★ **colmo:** unbelievable, incredible. *¡Encuentro el **col-***

FOODS / COMIDA

ají: either a hot pepper or hot sauce.

aliado: a ham and cheese sandwich.

anticucho: a shish kebab, skewer.

arrollado primavera: a Chinese spring roll.

cabritas: popcorn.

callampa: mushrooms.

carne al disco: a type of BBQ that is cooked in a round disc.

cazuela: a stew made from beef or chicken, potatoes, pumpkin and other vegetables, with a thin broth.

cecina: a general term for any lunch meat.

charqui: beef jerky.

chirimoya: sour sop fruit.

chirimoya alegre: a flavor often used in ice cream and yogurt that is a combination of chirimoya and orange.

choclo: corn.

chunchules: cow innards that are grilled and served at typical Chilean asados and parrilladas.

cochayuyo: a rust colored algae from the ocean, boiled and served in salads and stews.

completo: a hot dog loaded with everything, generally tartar sauce, chopped tomato and mayonnaise.

crudo: a steak tartare dish served with chopped onions and bread, and "cooked" with lemon juice.

cuchufli: a wafer cookie sold by street vendors.

delicia: a cookie filled with different flavors of marmalade.

durazno: a peach.

frutilla: strawberry.

italiano: a hot dog with mayonnaise, diced tomato and avocado paste.

jaiba: crab.

lomito: sliced pork most often used in sandwiches.

machas: razor clams.

malva: just like marshmallow, but thicker, less spongy.

malvabisco: marshmallow.

FOODS / COMIDA, *continued*

manjar: a typical caramel type sweet that is used in candies, pastries and all types of desserts.

mantecado: a butter cookie.

merquén: a spice used to give things a hot flavor to them, similar to chili powder.

mil hojas: a typical pastry dough used for different types of desserts.

ostiones: scallops.

palomitas: popcorn.

pan amasado: a typical Chilean bread often baked in a brick oven.

pan batido: another name for *pan marraqueta*.

pan de molde: loaf bread.

pan francés: another term for *pan marraqueta.*

pan frica: a round type of bread used, for example, for hamburger buns.

pan hallulla: a typical Chilean bread round-shaped and extremely flat.

pan marraqueta: a type of bread shaped pretty closely to butt-cheeks.

pelayo: a type of chewy candy, most often made with milk.

pichanga: a plate of stuff to munch on such as olives, hams, cold cuts, pickled vegetables, etc.

pickle: different types of pickled vegetables, such as onions, cauliflower and carrots, not just the typical pickled cucumbers.

picoroco: a large barnacle that may be cooked and served; the meat is removed from the shell and eaten.

picoteo: appetizers, a plate of food to munch on.

prieta: blood sausage.

quesillo: a light, white cheese often served with salads.

salsa americana: although there are different variations of this common sauce, the closest comparison is relish.

salsa golf: sauce made of ketchup and mayonnaise.

vienesa: a hot dog.

***mo** que llegues tan tarde al trabajo!*

columpiar: to tease, make fun of someone.

comadrear: chat, gossip.

combo: a punch.

💣 **combo en la guata:** to jerk off, masturbate.

comer delante de los pobres: to do something in front of other people that makes them envious, for example, kiss or make out with your boyfriend/ girlfriend.

💣 **comerse a alguien:** to have sex.

¿Cómo andamos por casa?: what are you talking about, you're the same way!, isn't this the pot calling the kettle black.

como avión: everything good, going well.

como el hoyo: 1) a person that comes across to you as bad. 2) to not feel well.

como el loly: going poorly, not well, bad.

¿Cómo está el dragón?: how's the hangover?

como la mona: bad, terrible.

como la zorra: horrible, awful, bad. *Me fue **como la zorra** en química. Tengo que repetirla el próximo verano.*

como las huevas: with problems, complicated, in a mess.

como piojo: trashed, drunk. *Tomó tanto que terminó **como piojo**.*

¿Cómo te lo explico?: an expression used to fill a gap in the conversation while you think of how to properly express yourself.

como visita de doctor: fast, quick, in and out. *Voy a Santiago el próximo jueves, **como visita de doctor**, asi que vuelvo el viernes.*

★ **compadre:** dude.

completo: a hot dog loaded with everything , generally tartar sauce, chopped tomato and mayonnaise.

componer la caña: to help recover from a hangover.

comprar terreno: joking phrase to say someone fell, wiped out, literally "to purchase land". *Me caí frente a la municipalidad, **compré terreno.***

computín: anyone that uses the computer all the time. *Los* *niños hoy son súper **computínes**, saben N.*

comunacho: a leftist, communist.

con el poto a dos manos: scared shitless.

con la alita quebrada: literally "with a broken wing", recently divorced.

con los indios: hung over.

con tutti: with everything or all out. *Al principio, le dio un beso tímido, pero después fue **con tutti**.*

💣 **concha**: 1) pussy. 2) exclamation to express anger, such as Shit or Son of a bitch!

💣 **conchatumadre / conchasumadre:** 1) a mother fucker, a son of a bitch. *Ese **conchasumadre** tiene tres pololas.* 2) Shit!, Damn!, often used after you've hurt yourself, forgot something or something bad happened. ***¡Conchatumadre!** Se me quedó el pasaporte en casa.*

conchazo: to have a hard fall. *Me caí en la tina, me dí un tremendo **conchazo** en la pierna.*

concho: a bit, a tad. *Te queda un **concho** de la botella, para terminarlo.*

★ **condoro:** a screw-up, a mess. *Me mandé el medio **condoro** ayer con el jefe cuando le entregué el informe equivocado.*

💣 **conferencia de prensa:** a blowjob.

confort: toilet paper, name comes from the brand of toilet paper but now is used generically for any brand of toilet paper.

consecuente: to be a straight person, honest, correct.

constipado: a bad cold.

consultorio: small public health care centers for typical medical problems, are not generally used for emergency situations, a *posta* would be used for an emergency.

★ **copete:** any alcoholic beverage. *Se armó un carrete con harta comida y harto **copete**.*

★ **copeteada:** drunk.

★ **copetear:** to go out drinking.

copucha: gossip.

copuchar: to gossip.

copuchentear: to gossip.

copuchento: nosy, gossipy, in other people's business.

corchetera: stapler, other Spanish words are *abrochadora, engrapadora* and *grapadora*.

cornetero: a kiss-up.

correrse: to stand up, blow off, skip. *Estoy segura que va a* ***correrse****, siempre lo hace.*

[$] **cortando:** refers to how much money you make. *¿Cuánto estás* ***cortando*** *ahora, Juan?*

cortar el agua: to cut off from sex, often as a punishment. *Javier llegó tarde anoche así que su mujer le va a* ***cortar el agua***.

cortar el queque: to make a decision, one way or the other. *Ya por favor decídete, es necesario* ***cortar el queque.***

cortarse la leche: to lose interest in.

cosiaca: matter, subject, topic.

cosito/a: term of endearment for a loved one.

coso/a: 1) thingy. 2) a term of endearment for friends.

cototo: 1) cool, interesting, nice. 2) hard, difficult.

cototudo: 1) awesome, cool. 2) hard, difficult.

counter: same as the English usage. *En el* ***counter*** *de LAN hay que prechequearse.*

crack: an ace, expert in something, generally used in reference to soccer. *El* ***crack*** *David Beckham ya no está jugando tanto.*

cranear: to think about, analyze, work something out in your head. *Necesito* ***cranear*** *algo para esta noche así que te contesto mañana.*

creerse el hoyo del queque: to think you're the bees knees, the best.

★ **creerse la muerte:** to be extremely confident in one's self, to the point of arrogance. *Se operó y se ve regia,* ***¡Se cree la muerte!***

creído: vain, big-headed.

★ **cresta:** far away. *La casa de Paula queda en la* ***cresta*** *de la loma.*

crudo: a steak tartare dish served with chopped onions and bread, and "cooked" with lemon juice.

cuartear: to spy on someone who is naked but does not realize you are watching.

cuático: a "square" person, old-fashioned, narrow-minded, straightlaced, someone who overreacts because of their narrow-minded views.

cuatiquero: someone who makes a big scene of everything, melodramatic.

cuatro por cuatro (4 x 4): someone who is up for anything, similar to the all terrain vehicle that goes anywhere. *Me encanta su actitud, es una **4x4**.*

cuca: a Carabineros vehicle that is van size, used to lock up arrested protesters during riots.

cuchara: another word for heart.

cuchufleta: a well prepared lie usually to obtain some economic benefit.

cuchufli: a wafer cookie, shaped like a straw, sometimes filled with *manjar* and sold by street vendors.

cuco: the boogeyman.

★ **cueca:** the national Chilean folk dance.

cuentero: a liar, someone that makes stories up. *Jaime es súper **cuentero**, no hay que creerle mucho.*

cuento: a lie, a made up story. *Siempre que llega tarde a la oficina, inventa un **cuento** diferente.*

cuero: a hot body. *Tiene tremendo **cuero**, por eso era modelo de tv.*

cuero de chancho: thick-skinned, insults roll right off.

★ **cuestión:** thingy, thingamajig. *Ellos discutieron sobre una **cuestíon** pequeña.*

cueva: 1) ass. 2) luck. *Con **cueva** vamos a lograr el objetivo de venta este mes.*

cuevudo: lucky. *Se ganó un tremendo premio anoche, es súper **cuevúo**.*

★ **cuico/a:** snobby, stuck-up, often used in reference to someone of a higher social class.

💣 **culiado:** fucker, shithead, SOB, dickhead, depending on the context. Is often used to mean the person in question is a real huge dickhead.

💣 **culiar:** to fuck someone.

💣 **culión:** a fuck, a screw.

★ **culo:** ass, in other countries may refer specifically to the asshole, but in Chile the usage is in reference to the whole ass. *Mira el **culo** rico que tiene esa mina.*

culo a dos manos: worried about something that could happen.

cuma: low class, sleazy.

cumpleaños de monos: out of control situation, literally "a monkey's birthday".

curadito: drunk.

curado: 1) drunk, trashed, hammered. *Tomó tanto para las Fiestas Patrias que terminó raja de **curado**.* 2) kite string that is covered in shards of glass, to allow for kite dueling. The object is to use your kite string to cut the other person's string.

curahuilla: drunk.

curanto: a typical seafood stew from the Chiloé region.

★ **curarse:** to get drunk. *Ok, salgan pero sin **curarse**.*

D

★ **da lo mismo:** whatever, it doesn't matter, it's all the same.

¡dale!: okay, sure, go ahead.

dale no más: Go ahead!, Have at it!

dale con que las gallinas mean: to continue fighting a losing position, to the point of being hardheaded.

• dale con que las gallinas mean •

dar bola: to pay attention to, take into account.

dar boleto: to take into account, to pay attention to.

dar el filo: 1) to not give much attention to. 2) to end a relationship, break up with someone.

dar esférica: to pay attention to.

dar guaraca: a blowout in a sports event. *El Colo le **dio guaraca** a la U en el último partido.*

dar jugo: to annoy, bother, mess around with.

dar la hora: to be clueless.

dar la lata: to talk a lot.

dar la pasada: to give permission (for sex). *Estuve a punto de* ***dar la pasada****, Javier me encanta.*

dar paja: to feel lazy. *Me* ***da paja*** *ir a trabajar después de almorzar.*

dar pelota: to pay attention to, take into account. *Me cae mal, no le pienso* ***dar pelota****.*

darle color: to exaggerate, focus on unnecessarily or to blow out of proportion. *Ya pasó, deja de* ***darle color****, ya no vale la pena.*

darle un chiquitito: to wait a minute. *Te atiendo enseguida,* ***dame un chiquitito.***

dar el viejazo: when you are in pain (arms, legs, back...).

darse un conchazo: to fall down hard. *Si no tengo cuidado me voy a* ***dar un conchazo.***

💣 **darse un porrazo:** 1) to fall down hard. 2) to screw someone, have sex.

darse vuelta el mapa: to become extremely confused, make a mistake, literally "to turn the map upside down".

darselas de vivo/a: to pretend to know everything but to not really know.

de alla somos: Count me in!, in reference to a night out on the town with friends.

de cartón: false, a fake person, a liar.

de chincol a jote: a big flirt, a player.

de farra: out on the town, out partying. *Anoche me fui* ***de farra*** *con unos amigos.*

de las chacras: a country person, most often naïve.

de más: of course, obviously. *¿Vai a la fiesta mañana? ¡****De más*** *que sí!*

de medio pelo: vulgar, sleazy, trashy. *La tienda no es muy buena, se ve* ***de medio pelo.***

de parranda: out on the town, out partying. *Anoche estuve* ***de parranda*** *con unos amigos.*

de pe a pa: an expert, someone with deep knowledge.

de rompe y raja: immediately, right away without thinking.

de salón: ironic term to point out the foul language someone is using.

decir la F: to tell the truth, to give it straight.

dejar la embarrada: to make a mess of things. *Me gusta salir con ustedes, pero siempre **dejan la embarrá.***

★ **dejar la escoba:** 1) to screw off, causing problems or bothering others. 2) to royally screw things up, to cause a huge problem, make a mess of things. *Ayer, mi hermano **dejó la escoba** en el trabajo cuando le gritó al jefe.*

dejar pagando: to stand up, blow off. *No quiero ir, los voy a **dejar pagando**.*

dejar plantado: to stand someone up.

dejar tirado: to be stood up.

dejarme plop: see *quedarse plop.*

dejarse caer por ahí: to surprise someone with a visit.

• dejar la escoba •

del mundo de Bilz y Pap: a fantasy world, la-la land.

delantera: a woman's knockers, jugs. *Se puso implantes y quedó con tremenda* ***delantera****.*

delicia: a cookie filled with different flavors of marmalade.

denante: a bit ago, a while ago, before.

denso: bull-headed, pig-headed, hard-headed. *Siempre que nos reunimos se pone* ***denso****, no se llega a nada.*

desatinado: cross the line, out of place, say or do something socially unacceptable.

descrestarse: to exert a whole lot of force in something, for example, work or to buy a new car. *El pobre tipo* ***se descresta*** *trabajando cada día en dos turnos para mantener a su familia.*

★ **descueve:** awesome, cool, sweet, great. *Este fin de semana lo pasamos el* ***descueve*** *en casa de la Pame.*

despachar: to get rid of, throw out, dump a guy.

despotricar: to be extremely pissed off.

★ **desubicado/a:** out of place, cross the line, go too far.

día de pago de los bomberos: literally "firemen's pay day", phrase used to mean never, since all firemen are volunteers in Chile.

día del pico: never. *No termino nunca, el* ***día del pico*** *me voy a poder ir temprano a casa.*

diario: newspaper, literally "daily", another common Spanish word is *periodico*.

días R: a woman's period. *Me siento pésima, estoy en los* ***días R****.*

dicharachero: a person who jokes a lot and always seems to be happy.

diente largo: extremely hungry, famished.

dije: correct, charming, nice.

💣 **dirigirse al público:** a blow job.

💣 **dirigirse el país:** a blow job.

disfrutar la vida a concho: to live to the max, enjoy life to the fullest.

CLOTHING / ROPA

abuelaless: granny style women's underwear.

andar a lo gringo: going commando, to not wear underwear.

beatle: a turtleneck shirt.

buzo: sweatpants.

chala: a sandal.

chaleco: an open type of sweater, similar or the same as a cardigan.

chomba: sweater.

chupalla: a straw hat used by *huasos*.

colaless: G-string underwear, a thong.

colleras: cuff links, other Spanish words are *gemelos* and *yuntas*.

hilo dental: a G-string, V-string or any other type of tiny underwear.

montgomery: a rain overcoat.

polera: a t-shirt.

poncho: a wool blanket used by *huasos* as a type of jacket.

slip: men's underwear, specifically briefs.

sostén: a bra, other words used in Spanish are *corpiño* and *brassiere*.

tato: shoe.

terno: a business suit.

tillas: tennis shoes, short for *zapatillas*.

vestón: a formal jacket, also a jacket used by students as part of their uniform.

zunga: 1) a Speedo type men's bathing suit 2) underwear briefs.

dividendo: a mortgage payment.

dodge pata: by foot, walking. *No creo que vaya al concierto, me tendría que devolver en **Dodge pata**.*

donde el diablo perdió el poncho: Timbuktu, really far away, literally "where the Devil lost his poncho".

donde las papas queman: the happening place, the center of attention.

donde pica la jaiva: a dangerous, sketchy place.

doragua: refers to the brand

of beer Dorada in an insulting way by combining the name of the beer with the word *agua*, to say the beer is watered down.

dormir a pata suelta: to be deep asleep.

dormir ensillado: to sleep in your clothes, fully dressed.

dormir la mona: to sleep off a hangover.

dormir raja: dead asleep. *Me acosté súper cansada,* ***dormí raja****.*

down: depressed, down.

durar menos que un candy: to not last long. *El pastel estaba muy rico, me* ***duró menos que un candy****.*

durazno: a peach, another Spanish word is *melocotón.*

E

echar: to break something.

echar el poto a las moras: to back out of, to cancel.

echar la chorea: to look for a fight, argument.

echar la choriada: to challenge someone to a fight.

echar la foca: to scold someone. *Llegué súper tarde a trabajar, estoy segura que me van a* ***echar la foca****.*

echar la jineta: pass the buck, load up your work on your employees. *Es un abusador, siempre está* ***echando sus jinetas*** *encima.*

echar la talla: to have fun with friends hanging out.

💣 **echar un pato:** to screw, have sex.

echarse a volar: to scram, beat it, get out of town.

echarse al pollo: to leave, go away.

echarse al trajín: to have sex with a different person each time.

echarse el pollo: to skip out, leave, go away.

echarse la yegua: when you are so relaxed or tired that you do not want to move.

echárselo: 1) to fail a class at school *Me* ***eché*** *cálculo así que voy a estar estudiando en verano.* 2) to break something.

échate al pollo: Leave!, Get out of here! *No quiero que estés acá, **échate al pollo** no más.*

ecolecua: exactly, that's it, you got it.

el año del loly: never.

el día del níspero: never.

el hachazo: hangover.

el Mercado Central: a place to get seafood, but it is often a joke that you only go there when you're hung over, to help recover from the hangover. Also, since several seafoods are believed to be aphrodisiacs, people may laugh when you mention you went to the Mercado Central, thinking that it was to increase your sexual prowess.

el Persa: a huge flea market in Santiago.

el que la lleva: the leader.

el que nace chicharra muere cantando: phrase used to say that once a person is a certain way, they will always be the same, people never change.

embalado: wrapped up in something, well-versed. *Hemos avanzado mucho, estamos **embalaos**.*

★ **embarrada:** a mess of things, a screw-up.

emo: abbreviation of emotional and is one of the main Urban Tribes, the typical *emo* uses tight clothes, skater shoes, lots of piercings and sideburns, generally emotional people, introspective, introverted.

empalarse: to freeze.

emparafinado: a bit drunk.

empelotado: angry, pissed off. *Rodrigo hace todo mal, me tiene **empelotado**.*

empiernado: to be accompanied.

empinar el codo: to tip back the elbow, as in beer/alcohol drinking.

empotarse: to be in a relationship only for the sex.

★ **emputecer:** to be pissed off, angry. *Me **emputecé** ver como abusan de los más débiles.*

emputecido: pissed off, furious.

en calidad de bulto: wiped out, either from drinking or extremely sick, useless.

en cana: in prison.

en denante: before, but in the recent past, recently, use of phrase comes across as extremely poor education.

en la cresta: far off, Timbuktu, in the middle of nowhere.

★ **en la punta del cerro:** really far away, Timbuktu. *Ahora vivo en la Florida, eso es* ***en la punta del cerro****.*

★ **en lo absoluto:** Not at all!

en pana: a stalled or broken down car. *Mira Pame, estoy* ***en pana*** *así que no alcanzo a llegar a la hora.*

★ **en pelota:** naked. *Mi hijo siempre anda* ***en pelota*** *cuando estamos en la playa.*

en una de esas: perhaps, maybe.

en upa: to carry someone in your arms.

encachado: attractive, handsome, eye-catching in reference to people, places or things. *El modelo es bien* ***encachado****.*

encalillado: with a lot of debts.

encargarse: expression to emphasize that something is too much. *¡Tengo un dolor de cabeza que te lo* ***encargo****!*

encatrarse: to climb into bed to have sex.

enchúfate plancha de campo: pay attention, catch up in the conversation.

enchular: to fix up, to dress up. *Se acaba de* ***enchular*** *en la peluquería, se ve regia.*

encontrón: an argument, a run-in.

endeble: weak, flimsy.

★ **ene or N:** 1) a long time. *Me costó* ***ene*** *aprender inglés. Estuvimos* ***N*** *rato esperando la micro.* 2) a whole lot of something. *Hay* ***ene*** *trabajo en las mineras con el precio de cobre tan alto.*

enfermo: extremely. *El Farkas es* ***enfermo*** *de rico.*

★ **enganchar:** to connect with a person, group or conversation. *Los estudiantes estaban discutiendo el futuro del cobre en la economía chilena y me quedé tan* ***enganchado*** *con el tema que escribí mi tesis sobre ello.*

engañito: small gift.

engrupiento: tricky, sly, slick to the point of lying.

★ **engrupir:** to trick or deceive. *Me va a tocar*

engruprir en la presentación de la tarde, no sé mucho del tema.

enrollado: wrapped up in, involved in to the point of inventing explanations or theories.

★ **ensalada chilena:** a salad of tomatoes, onion and cilantro.

entrar a caminar: to get going, leave, move in.

entrar agua al bote: to get drunk.

★ **entrete**: fun, cool, an abbreviation of *entretenido.*

envenado: extremely pissed off, angry as all get out.

era grande el finado: phrase said when someone is using an oversized piece of clothing. *Me prestaron una chaqueta y **era más grande el finado**, me queda enorme.*

es bueno mirar el carné de vez en cuando: phrase used to point out that someone is living a lifestyle younger than their age, and that they need to act their age.

escupo: term that means spit used in reference to the brand of beer Escudo, to insult the quality of the beer.

escurrido: someone who takes more than what the other is offering. May be in a relationship or with money.

espeso: thick-headed, annoying, not nice.

espornocu: joke used when a zit breaks out on your face. The zit is called an *espornocu* which comes from *es por no culiar* and means that you haven't been laid in a while, so the zit is caused by lack of sex. *Tengo la cara muy fea, llena de **espornocu**.*

está pedido: there is nothing to do to help him in a specific situation, his destiny is already written. *Lo evaluaron pésimo en su trabajo, yo creo que **está pedido**.*

está que arde: the best, great, awesome.

estar a la sombra: to be in jail.

estar apenas: to be full, stuffed.

estar apestado: to be tired of something that occurs repeatedly. *¡**Estoy apestadísima** con tanta pega... no me alcanza el tiempo!*

estar botado: to be easy, as in an exam. *La prueba*

*estaba **botada**, me fue muy bien.*

estar botella: single, without a romantic partner. *Voy a **estar botella** este fin de semana; Julio anda de viaje por trabajo.*

estar cabezón: too much alcohol in a drink. *El copete **está cabezón**, por favor, pásame la coca cola.*

estar cachúa: to be suspicious of. ***Estoy cachúa** con la Carolina porque cacho que me está mintiendo.*

💣 **estar cagado:** 1) fucked, in trouble. 2) scared shitless.

estar caleta: to be fed up.

estar cayendo los patos asados: to be extremely hot weather. *En Temuco hizo mucho calor, **están cayendo los patos asados**.*

★ **estar chato:** 1) to be stuffed after eating. 2) to be tired of something, fed up with. *Andrea **está chata** con los niños ya que lleva tres meses encerrada en casa con ellos.* 3) dead tired, wiped out.

estar chocha: to be pleased, proud, happy with.

estar choclo: to be finished, ready, done.

estar como el pico: to be bad off, to feel bad. *No dormí nada, voy a estar todo el día **como el pico**.*

estar como las pelotas: to be bad off, from being sick, depressed or whatever.

estar como piojo: to be extremely drunk or high, wasted.

estar como tuna: to be like new, in perfect condition. *En las vacaciones descansé mucho, **estoy como tuna**.*

estar de boni: to be a hot babe. *Mira la de verde al final de la barra; **está de boni**.*

estar de cajón: to be clear or obvious.

estar diciendo: same as *de más*.

estar donde calienta el sol: to change positions depending on what's best for you, on how the winds blow.

estar en la pitilla: to be extremely thin.

★ **estar en otra:** to not be focused, to not pay attention. *No me pesca el jefe, se nota que **está en otra**, preparándose para la reunión con los inversionistas.*

HUEV-

Welcome to the most useful page in the book.

agarrar para el hueveo: 1) to tease someone, to jerk their chain 2) to not take a romantic relationship seriously, a fling, just mess around with.

ahuevonado: dumb, stupid, idiotic, so stupid that what is obvious to everyone else, he/she doesn't realize.

andar a huevear a los pacos: to tell someone to go bother someone else, literally "go screw with the pigs (as in cops)".

bueno/a para el hueveo: this phrase has different meanings when used in reference to a man or a woman. When used to describe a man, it means that he loves to go out and drink, but in reference to a female, it means that she is slutty or easy.

como las huevas: with problems, complicated, in a mess.

hacerse el huevón: to play dumb, make like you don't know what's going on.

huevada: something foolish, dumb, a waste of time.

huevas: a guy's balls or nuts.

huevear: 1) screw around, mess around, in a positive sense 2) to bother, annoy.

huevear más que una puta embarazada: to really bug the shit out of someone, literally "to bother more than a pregnant whore".

hueveo: 1) a fun, entertaining situation 2) something annoying, a pain in the ass.

huevón: 1) a dumbshit, an idiot 2) something like buddy, dude or shithead, used among close friends.

huevón culiado: a motherfucking son-of-a-bitch.

huevonaje: a group of *huevones*.

huevoncito: an insulting, ironic way to refer to someone, as in "that little dumbshit".

huevonear: to cuss someone out.

mata de huevas: an annoying person, someone that you can't even put up with.

HUEV-, *continued*

puta la huevada: shit, son of a bitch, motherfucker, an all inclusive statement after something bad occurs.

¿Qué huevada?: What the hell?

saco de huevas: a dumb, useless, foolish person.

una tracalá de huevones: a crowd of people.

¿Y qué huevada?: What the hell's going on?

estar entre Tongoy y Los Vilos: 1) halfway between drunk and sober, buzzed 2) disoriented, confused.

estar fiambre: dead.

estar finito: ironic term to say that someone swears a lot.

estar happy: buzzed, but not yet drunk.

★ **estar harto:** to be fed up with, to have had enough of, tired of.

estar hecho una bosta: to be worthless, completely worn out.

estar helado: to be broke, penniless.

estar la zorra: to be a messed up, chaotic situation.

estar Liz Taylor: ready-to-go, finished. ***Estamos Liz Taylor*** *con el carrete este sábado.*

💣 **estar papo:** short for "está para ponérselo", means that a woman is hot, or attractive, literally "she's for put ting it in". *Es muy guapa,* ***está papo***.

estar para el gato: to be bad off, extremely sick. *Tomé tanto que voy a* ***estar todo el día pa'l gato.***

estar para la goma: to be sick.

[$] **estar pato:** to be flat broke.

estar picado: mad, pissed off at someone.

💣 **estar que corto las huinchas:** 1) to want to fuck, horny as hell. 2) to be anxious waiting for something to happen. ***Estoy que corto las huinchas*** *por ir al concierto.*

💣 **estar raja:** 1) wiped out, tired. 2) trashed, wasted, shitfaced.

estar reventado: to be exhausted, completely worn out, wiped out. *Trabajé hasta muy tarde así que* ***estoy reventado.***

★ **estar zeta:** to be dead tired.

estrujarse de la risa: to laugh too much.

F

★ **facha:** physical appearance, look. *Me encanta como se ve Naty, tiene una tremenda* ***facha.***

facho: from the right, politically.

[$] **factura:** a receipt for business purposes that allows you to recover the Value Added Tax (IVA is the Spanish abbreviation) paid on any purchase, most often used for company or business expenses.

falopa: drugs, cocaine.

💣 **falta de vitamina P:** a lack of sex, literally "lack of vitamin P", which stands for *pico* or dick. Often used when you run across someone that needs to get laid so she'll loosen up a bit. *Está muy pesada hoy, le* ***falta mucha vitamina P.***

faltar gramos para el kilo: slow, stupid, missing a few screws.

faltar la P: to be almost ready, just a minute. *Esperame un poco, me* ***falta la P.***

faltar palos para el puente: slow, stupid, missing a few screws.

fanfarrón: rum with orange Fanta.

★ **fanschop:** a draft beer mixed with orange flavored soda (generally Fanta).

farriando clase: skipping class, blowing off class.

★ **feliz de la vida:** happy as a clam. *Como está de vacaciones, anda* ***feliz de la vida.***

★ **fiaca:** laziness. *Amanecí con la* ***fiaca*** *viva.*

fichar: 1) to correctly identify someone's characteristics. 2) to categorize someone as a certain way.

filete: awesome, good, cool. *El recital estuvo muy bueno,* ***filete.***

★ **filo:** 1) it's over, we're finished. 2) it's no longer open for discussion.

finito: a delicate man, gay.

fisco: the government.

fito: nickname for a Fiat 600 model car.

flaco/a: friend, buddy, pal. *¿Oye **flaco**, tomamos un copete hoy?*

flacuchento: extremely thin.

★ **flaite:** ghetto, low class, disgusting.

flato: a belch.

fletiar: to beat or hit.

💣 **fletito:** gay, homo.

💣 **fleto:** gay, homo.

★ **flojera:** laziness.

★ **flojo:** a slacker. *Es súper **flojo**, no le gusta hacer nada.*

florero: someone who always needs to be the center of attention.

★ **fome:** boring, blah, dull. *Esta clase es muy **fome** y el profesor horrible.*

Fonasa: the public health care system.

★ **fonda:** any type of party that occurs to celebrate the 18th of September, usually includes *empanadas, chicha, pipeño* and other typical Chilean food and drink, as well as rodeo activities, typical Chilean dress, and other games.

💣 **fosforito:** a person that gets horny quickly, doesn't take them much to get going.

Franklin: a neighborhood in Santiago that has a daily flea market where you can find all kinds of things (often junk) for sale. If you ever find your car missing a side mirror, or a hubcap, for example, there's a good chance you could find it for sale a couple days later in Franklin.

fregado: a complicated person, often negative, there's always a but to the situation. *Los protestantes frente la Moneda son iguales de **fregados**.*

freir la pescada: to make up lies.

fritanga: a place that serves different types of fried foods.

frito: screwed.

frutilla: strawberry, another Spanish word is *fresa*.

fulano/a: Joe Blow. *Me encontré con ese **fulano** bien feo del cuarto piso.*

funar: it doesn't work, fail.

G

gallada: what the normal populace, or the crowd, believes.

galleta: the extra person that's included even though they really don't belong, in sports for example it would be the person that stands on the field but doesn't do anything.

★ **gallo/a:** guy, dude/chick, babe. *Ya poh **galla**, avanza, tenemos que salir.*

[$] **gamba:** 1) a huge foot. *¡Mira las **gambas** de ese gallo!* 2) a 100 peso coin. *Quiero comprar un dulce, dame una **gamba**.* 3) 100 thousand Chilean pesos.

gancho: dude, buddy. *Ya **gancho**, nos juntamos mañana temprano.*

ganso: 1) dumb, idiot, retard. *Es súper **ganso**, nunca entiende nada.* 2) friendly term used among friends for dude, man, pal, guy.

★ **garabato:** a cuss word, swear word.

garra blanca: fans of the Colo Colo soccer team. *En el estadio es emocionante escuchar a la **Garra Blanca**.*

garrafa: a 5-liter bottle, the equivalent of about 1.25 gallons, most often used for wine or *chicha*.

garreros: fans of Colo Colo.

gasfiter: a plumber. *Se me echaron a perder las llaves del baño, necesito urgente un **gasfiter**.*

Gasparín: literally Casper the Friendly Ghost, means light-skinned, extremely white. *Fui a la piscina hoy y parezco **Gasparín**.*

gastarse parejo: bisexual.

gastos comunes: condo fee, monthly maintenance expenses for an apartment.

gato de chalet: lazy, spoiled.

gauchada: a favor. *Necesito que me ayudes, hazme una **gauchada**.*

género: cloth.

Gilberto: fool, dummy.

golpeadito: a shot of liquor.

💣 **gomas:** hooters, jugs, large breasts. *Los hombres viven mirando las **gomas** de María.*

gordo/a: affectionate term used for loved ones, especially with or in reference to your kids, or to your husband/wife or partner.

gorrear: to cheat on your partner. *Ni se te ocurra **gorrear** a Francisco en vacaciones.*

grado 1: a kiss.

grado 2: making out.

💣 **grado 3:** sex

💣 **grado 4:** anal sex

💣 **grado 7:** this would be *grado 3* and *grado 4* at the same time.

greda: a type of clay used to make dishes and pots, that conduct heat well, so are often used for baking, or serving food to keep it hot.

★ **gringo:** a term to refer to foreigners, most often English speakers, or even just Americans.

★ **gringolandia:** slang for the United States of America, literally "Land of Gringos". This term is in no way insulting.

grosso: good, cool. *El completo de Dominó era **grosso**.*

★ **grupiento:** lying or misleading in an effort to achieve or obtain something, for example to sleep with someone. *Juan es más **grupiento** que la cresta; la última vez dejó la embarrá en la oficina.*

grupo: lies. *No me cuentes nada más, apuesto que es puro **grupo** lo que dices.*

★ **guácala:** Yuck!, Gross! Disgusting!, alternate spelling is *wuakala*.

guacha: a hot chick, but trashy looking too.

guachaca: trashy, sleazy, low-class.

💣 **guachalomo:** a dick.

guachipetiar: to rob or take from.

guachita: a hot chick.

guachón: an attractive, hot guy. *Me encanta Javier es un tremendo **guachón**.*

★ **guagua:** a baby, another typical Spanish word is *bebé*.

*Hace pocos días nació la **guagua** y andan súper felices.*

guagua que no llora, no mama: whoever remains quiet will not achieve anything or get much, literally means "baby that doesn't cry, doesn't breast feed".

guaguita: a tiny baby.

guailón: large, goofy, a doofus.

guanaco: 1) a llama-like animal. 2) the tank-like vehicle with a mounted water cannon, used by the Carabineros police for crowd control and breaking up riots. The name comes from the animal which has a tendency to spit at people.

guapetón: an elegant, attractive, well-dressed man.

guardarse en el sobre: to go to bed, go lay down. *Si no tengo nada más que hacer, sólo hay que **guardarse en el sobre.***

guarifaifa: a thingy.

guaripola: an ace, expert in a topic.

guarisnaque: any type of drink that you are not sure of the contents, for example an alcoholic beverage.

guasquiado: more than a little drunk.

★ **guata:** tummy.

guata de lija: a suck-up, brown-noser.

guata de perro: someone that will eat anything, literally "a dog's tummy".

guatear: screwed up, messed up.

guatecallo: a suck-up, brown-noser.

guatero: a bag of wine that comes inside boxed wine, always an extremely cheap wine.

guatitas: a typical Chilean dish of sliced cow's stomach stewed for a long time and served with any of a variety of sauces.

guatón: 1) a million Chilean pesos. *Se ganó la lotería y se llevó 15 **guatones**.* 2) term of endearment, between couples or also used for a child or baby. 3) a fat person.

güergüero: throat. *El agua que tomé estaba tan helada que me dolió el **güergüero**.*

H

hablar cabezas de pescado: to make stuff up, tell lies.

hacer buenas migas: to become good friends. *Conocí a alguien la otra noche,* ***hicimos buenas migas****.*

hacer el dos: to accompany someone.

💣 **hacer el favor:** to have sex with someone, to screw someone.

hacer gancho: to be a matchmaker.

hacer la cama: secretly ambush someone, screw them over. *Si no estoy atenta, me van a* ***hacer la cama****, no son muy derechos.*

hacer la chancha: to play hooky, to skip school.

hacer la cimarra: to skip school.

hacer la corta: to be rushed, in a hurry, quickly. *Voy al mall a comprar unos vasos, prometo* ***hacer la corta.***

hacer la pata: a kiss-up, a brown-noser.

hacer la previa: to have a couple drinks to get things going before heading out for the night.

hacer pataleta: to create a scandal, especially over something inconsequential, for example, a kid that starts screaming because his mom won't buy him a candy at the grocery store.

hacer pichí: to pee.

★ **hacer sandwich:** to take vacation days when a holiday falls on a Tuesday, Wednesday or Thursday, extending the time off so the vacation includes the weekend, for example taking a vacation day on Monday, when the holiday is on Tuesday. For one day's vacation, you get a 4-day weekend.

★ **hacer tuto:** to sleep. *Tengo sueño, voy a* ***hacer tuto.***

hacer una vaca: to collect money, put money in a communal pot.

hacerla cortita: to make it fast, do something quickly.

hacerla de oro: to do something well, but may also be used ironically to say that you really screwed it up. *La* ***hizo de oro****, chocó un auto estacionado y ahora tiene que pagar caleta.*

hacerlo para allá: to move something from one place to another. *Por favor, corre la silla, **hacela pá allá.***

hacerse bolsa: completely wiped out, completely dead, from being tired or alcohol.

hacerse el cucho: to pretend to not remember something that was promised, for instance, to say you will lend money, but then pretend that you forgot you promised the money. *Para él es fácil **hacerse el chucho**, así no se compromete a nada.*

hacerse el huevón: to play dumb, make like you don't know what's going on.

hacerse el lindo: to act charming trying to get a woman's attention.

hacerse la cara: to put on makeup.

hacerse una friega con el carné: phrase used to point out that someone is living a lifestyle younger than their age, and that they need to act their age.

★ **harto:** a lot of something. *Hoy el profe dio **harta** tarea para la casa.*

hasta las masas: full of something, pissed off, lots of stuff to do. *Tengo mucha pega, estoy **hasta las masas**.*

hasta más: even more than.

hasta que las velas no ardan: until the very end.

Hawaian closet: an extremely pale person.

hay una araña en el baño: phrase used to say that the bathroom stinks because someone just finished there. *Nadie debe entrar; **hay una araña en el baño**.*

★ **heavy:** 1) a grave, difficult, touch and go situation. *Cuando la Jessica se cayó del balcón del cuarto piso eso sí que fue **heavy**.* 2) cool, great, awesome. *El concierto en Viña fue **heavy**.*

hechizo: hand-made.

hecho bolsa: wiped out, destroyed, completely worn out or run down.

★ **hediondo:** stinky, smelly.

hijo de tigre: an expert like his father.

★ **hilo dental:** a G-string, V-string or any other type of tiny underwear, literally "floss".

CAGAR

Welcome to the second most useful page in the book.

a cagar: to the end, all out, all the way.

a cagar no más: damn the consequences.

andar a cagarse: to tell someone to fuck off.

cagado: stingy, tight-fisted, especially in reference to money.

cagado de la cabeza: nuts, crazy.

cagado de la risa: dying of laughter.

cagado del mate: nuts, screwed in the head.

cagar: 1) to take a shit 2) to be amazed, to die for 3) to fuck over 4) to be fucked up, really messed up 5) nuts, crazy, off your rocker 6) screwed, messed up, over with.

cagarla: to fuck up, screw up.

cagaste: you missed your chance.

carretero a cagarse: a full out, extreme party animal.

estar cagado: 1) fucked, in trouble 2) scared shitless.

mandar cagadas: to fuck up, screw something up royally.

más cagado que palo de gallinero: broke, poor, bad off.

ni cagando: no fucking way.

nica / ni ca: short for *ni cagando.*

quedar la cagada / quedarse para la cagada: to be a messed up or fucked up situation.

ser cagado: miserly, stingy, cheap.

si la cago me avisas: when you know for sure that you screwed up.

hinchar: to bug, bother.

hocicón: a blabbermouth.

holi: Hey!, Hi!

hombre mosca: term used to describe someone that always makes a mess of things. *No hay caso, como siempre el **hombre mosca**.*

hospital: in Chile the word hospital refers specifically to public hospitals, where the level of care is generally lower than in a *clínica*, which are more upscale and privately run.

huachito carnuo: a phrase used by women to describe a hot guy.

★ **huaso/a:** 1) a typical Chilean cowboy or country person. *Para las Fiestas Patrias los niños se visten de **huasos** en el colegio.* 2) refers to someone uneducated, simple or out of touch with city life.

• huaso •

💣 **hueco:** 1) superficial, stuck up. 2) gay.

★ 💣 **huevada:** something foolish, dumb, a waste of time. *Deja de hacer esas **huevadas**.*

huevas: a guy's balls or nuts.

★ 💣 **huevear:** 1) screw around, mess around, in a positive sense. *Me encantó **huevear** en la fiesta.* 2) to bother, annoy. *Deja de **huevearme**; quiero estudiar.*

💣 **huevear más que una puta embarazada:** to really bother the shit out of someone, literally "to bother more than a pregnant whore".

💣 **hueveo:** 1) a fun, entertaining situation. *¡Estaba bueno el hueveo en la fiesta!* 2) something annoying, a pain in the ass. *Va a ser un **hueveo** terminar esta pega antes del viernes.*

★ 💣 **huevón:** 1) a dumbshit, an idiot. 2) something like buddy or dude, used among close friends.

💣 **huevón culiado:** a motherfucking son-of-a-bitch.

huevonaje: a group of *huevones*.

💣 **huevoncito:** an insulting, ironic way to refer to someone, as in "that little dumbshit".

huevonear: to cuss someone out.

huincha: a flexible measuring tape, generally made of cloth or flimsy paper.

humita: mashed corn, wrapped in a corn husk and cooked, often served with sugar sprinkled on top.

I

★ **igual:** anyway, in any event. ***Igual**, voy a tener que ir al banco.*

impeque: short for *impecable*, impeccable, perfect.

importar un comino: to not care about, to not be important. *Lo que tu pienses me **importa un comino**.*

importar un pito: to not care about, to not be important. *Me **importa un pito** tu opinión.*

💣 **importar una raja:** to not give a shit.

indio: fans of the Colo Colo soccer team.

indio pícaro: typical wooden statues of Mapuche indians that when lifted up have their private parts pop out.

inflar: to take into account, include. *Si no me vas a **inflar**, no te cuento nada.*

iñi piñi: tiny, miniscule. *Mi sueldo es **iñi piñi**, no me alcanza para vivir.*

inoperante: lazy. *No sirve para nada, es un **inoperante**.*

inpajaritable: definitively, without a doubt.

insolente: insolent, out of place, not respectful. *Daniel fue **insolente** con sus tatas.*

inteligente: indirect way of saying that someone is ugly, similar to "has a great personality" in English.

invocar a guajardo: a savage vomit, severe barfing, much more than other *guajardos.*

ir a la charla: to piss, for guys. *Esperanos acá, vamos a **ir a la charla** y volvemos.*

ir a las casitas: to go to the bathroom. *Tengo que **ir a las casitas**, ya no aguanto.*

ir al pipiroom: to go to the bathroom.

ir como el pico: to turn out poorly, to not go well.

ir como la zorra: to turn out poorly, to not go well.

ir de galleta: to be added on almost as an afterthought, to replace someone else, for example on a sports team.

ir de paracaidista: to show up uninvited.

irse a freir monos al África: to get the hell out of here, screw off. *Estoy harto de ti. ¿Por qué no te **vas a freir monos al África**?*

irse a la cresta: to go all wrong. *No pudimos ir de paseo, los planes se **fueron a la cresta.***

irse a las pailas: to not go the way something was planned, to turn out poorly.

irse al chancho: to go overboard, too much, as in spending money. *Cárgalo a mi cuenta, pero no te **vayai al chancho.***

💣 **irse cortado:** to cum, to have an orgasm.

irse de tollo: to let the tongue slip, let something escape.

irse en la mala: to react badly to something.

irse en la volada: to cross the line, to go beyond the acceptable.

irse por el aro: to not eat all day. *Trabajamos tanto que me **fui por el aro**.*

[$] **Isapre:** stands for *Instituciones de Salud Previsional*, and refers to private institutions that manage health care plans.

italiano: a hot dog with mayonnaise, diced tomato and avocado paste (the red, white and green of the Italian flag).

J

jaiba: crab, other Spanish words are *juey* and *cangrejo*.

jaivón: a rich person.

jalar: to sniff cocaine.

jale: a line of cocaine.

jalisco: someone that always has to be right.

jalisco zapata si no pierde empata: phrase to describe someone that can never lose, they will keep arguing until you give up, or a tie is declared, they are always right.

jarana: party. *Me encanta la **jarana**, aunque no tenga tanto aguante.*

jetón: dumbass, idiot. *Este **jetón** habla tanta tontera que lo detesto.*

jote: 1) someone that chases women, a vulture. 2) red wine with Coca Cola.

jotear: to chase after someone with a sexual goal in mind. *Miguel no deja de **jotear** a Pilar.*

Juanita tres cocos: tomboy.

juegue: dare.

jugoso: 1) a jokester. *José es súper **jugoso**, no para nunca.* 2) annoying, bothersome.

julepe: fear to do something

junior: a messenger, a person that runs all types of errands.

K

kardex: a filing cabinet.

kino acumulado: have been in a dry spell, no sex for a while. *No sé hasta cuando voy a estar con el **kino acumulado**.*

★ **kuchen:** a pastry or cake, comes from the German word for pastry, and the German culture's strong influence in Chile.

L

★ **la cagó:** 1) awesome, sweet, cool, well done. 2) crap, poorly done. *2) Definitivamente **la cagó**, no sabía nada al respecto.*

la dura: the truth.

la firme: the truth. *Si no me dices **la firme**, no te doy permiso.*

la media cueva: a whole lot of good luck. *Consiguió un buen trabajo, tiene **la media cueva.***

la Miss: a teacher, generally of kindergarten, nursery or elementary school.

★ **la muerte:** excellent, cool, the "ultimate".

la pelada: reference to several people dying at once, often in threes. *En el barrio pasó **la pelá**, ya se han muerto 3 personas.*

★ 💣 **la raja:** amazing, fun, fantastic, awesome, the shit.

la Roja: term used for the Chilean national soccer team. *Le tengo harta fe a **la Roja** en el Mundial.*

la selección: a reference to the Chilean national team in a sport, most often referring to soccer.

la tía rica: a government run pawn shop, literally the rich aunt. *Estoy tan endeudada que voy a tener que ir donde **la Tía Rica**.*

la U: at school, at college. *Me habría encantado terminar **la U**.*

la última chupada del mate: the best of the best. *Se compró un auto y ahora se cree **la última chupá del mate.***

La Vega: a daily outdoor market that offers fruits and vegetables at wholesale prices.

la zorra: awesome, kick-ass.

lacho: a womanizer, a player, a skirt-chaser, a guy that just plays with women.

ladillar: to bother.

ladrar: to bark at, bitch out, complain at. *Parece que se levantó con el pie izquierdo, no ha dejado de **ladrar**.*

lagartijear: to lay in the sun. *Me encanta **lagartijear** en vacaciones.*

lanza: a thief. *El centro está lleno de **lanzas**, hay que tener cuidado.*

★ **lata:** boring, no fun, nothing of consequence. *Que **lata** volver al trabajo, quisiera seguir de vacaciones.*

latero/a: boring, dull, no substance. *Habla demasiado y no dice nada, es un **latero**.*

latoso: a boring person.

lechuza: fan of the Universidad de Chile soccer team.

legal: the right way, the correct way.

lenteja: a slow person, not real motivated. *Es súper **lenteja**, no se apura nunca.*

lerda: slow, not able to do something well. *Es muy **lerda** para tejer.*

★ **leseo:** to bug or tease someone in a joking manner.

★ **leseras:** foolishness. *Deja de decir **leseras**, eres un pesado.*

lesiando: screwing around, bugging.

DIETS / DIETAS

Here's a fun list of Chilean diets that you can try... you are guaranteed to lose weight! I actually attempted to translate these into English, but they lose too much in the translation. Here's one example, just to give you an idea of how to understand these. Read them with some Chilean friends...

dieta del lagarto: literally "the lizard's diet", the lizard's diet is to *comer poco y culiar harto* or eat little and fuck a lot (see, it sounds better in Spanish).

dieta de Andrés: un polvo al derecho y otro al revés.

dieta de la hormiga: una tras otra.

dieta de la iguana: la misma del lagarto pero con mas ganas.

dieta de la lagartija: primero con la madre y después con la hija.

dieta de la sandía: de noche y de día.

dieta del caballo: régimen para *adelgazar* a base de pura agua y paja.

dieta del gringo: se lo pone el jueves y se lo saca el domingo.

dieta del melón: siempre con el mismo huevón.

dieta del membrillo: chuparlo hasta sacarle brillo.

dieta del Padre Hurtado: darle hasta que duela.

dieta del pan y pollo: un tuto pallá otro pacá y pan pan.

dieta de la manzana: con la mamá y también con la hermana.

dieta de la María Antonieta: con una pata en el catre y la otra en la ampolleta.

dieta de la pantera: una pata en el volante y la otra en la guantera.

dieta del cemento: duro y parejo.

dieta del granjero: a puro polvo y paja.

dieta del milico: dejar de comer de todo menos pico.

dieta del león: no siempre con el mismo huevón.

leso: fool, dummy. *Es súper **leso**, hace solo tonteras.*

levantado de raja: person that believes he is important and tries to show that he is, but really isn't. *Me carga, por que es bonita es súper **levantada** de raja.*

levantar con el pie izquierdo: to get up on the wrong side of the bed.

levantar polvo: to have a heated argument.

librar: to leave, vacate the premises.

★ **licencia:** a doctor's note saying that you are sick and cannot work or study, often required by companies and schools to verify a person's absence is legitimate.

💣 **limpiar la alfombra:** to give oral sex to a woman, literally "to clean the carpet".

💣 **lingote:** an annoying SOB.

★ **listo:** finished, done, ready. *Ya, está todo **listo**.*

llamar a guajardo: to barf.

★ **llave:** the water faucet.

llevarla: to know a topic inside and out. *Paula es muy buena en Finanzas, ¡La **lleva**!*

llorar la carta: to tell a sob story to get what you need. *Rosa siempre me está **llorando la carta** para que le dé plata.*

llover a chuzo: raining cats and dogs. *Quedé empapada, está **lloviendo a chuzo**.*

loggia: a utility room in an apartment.

lolein: someone very young or someone older that acts or dresses young. *Mi tía es súper **lolein** con la ropa que usa.*

lolo/a: teenager, young person. *Los **lolos** jugaron al fútbol todo el día.*

lolosaurio: an old man that chases young women, the word is a combination of *lola* and *dinosaurio*. *La disco estaba llena de **lolosaurios**.*

★ **lomito:** sliced pork most often used in sandwiches.

★ **lomo a lo pobre:** a typical dish of beef, fried onions, and french fries, with a fried egg on top.

★ **loquillo/a:** term of endearment used with a friend. *Oye, **loquillo**, ¿vamos al parque?*

lorear: to watch, stare at, observe.

loro: a booger.

los cruzados: fans of the Universidad Católica soccer team.

loser/looser: a nerd.

★ [$] **luca:** a thousand *pesos. Préstame una **luca** para comprarme los diarios.*

lumear: to scold, reprimand. *Mi mamá me va a **lumear** por llegar tarde ayer.*

lumpen: polite way to say a low-class person. *En las protestas se ven solo **lúmpenes**, no gente que de verdad proteste.*

M

macabeo: a guy that does everything his wife or girlfriend orders; house-whipped.

maceteado: big-boned, large, generally a mildly insulting term, especially for women.

machas: razor clams, most often served *a la parmesana* which is still in the shell, with grated parmesan cheese on top, and baked.

machetear: beg money in the street.

machetero: someone that always borrows money from friends and relatives.

maestro chasquilla: someone that fixes everything, but always leaves it worse off, and never really knows what they are doing. *El tipo que contraté resulto ser un **maestro chasquilla**, me dejó la cagada con las cañerías.*

magister: a master's degree, other Spanish words are *maestría* or *master.*

mal del tordo: a woman that has skinny legs and a big ass.

mal pelado el chancho: to split up unevenly, for example, food.

mala leche: a person with bad intentions.

mala pata: bad luck.

mala tela: bad vibes, bad attitude.

malandrín: a delinquent, a bad person.

malas pulgas: grumpy.

malena: bad off, not good.

maleta: car trunk, another Spanish word is *baúl.*

MONEY, MONEY, MONEY, MOOOOO-NEY

AFP: stands for *Administradora de Fondo de Pensiones* and refers to private pension fund companies.

aguinaldo: an extra salary payment that companies make to employees for Chile's independence celebrations (*Fiestas Patrias*) or for Christmas.

andar al 3 y al 4: to have no money.

andar cortina: to have no money, broke.

andar en pelotillehue: to be without money.

andar pato: to be broke.

andar patricio: to not have any money.

andar salado: to be broke.

andar sin ni uno: to be without a cent, broke.

Arturo/Arturito: a 10 thousand *peso* bill, named for Arturo Pratt, the person on the bill.

bicicleta: financial concept when a person borrows money to pay previous debts and continues this indefinitely.

billete largo: well-off, loaded.

billullo: money, bucks, moola.

boleta: a basic receipt for purchases, which is different from a *factura*.

cartola: bank account statement.

chaucha: pocket change, very little, a small amount.

cortando: refers to how much money you make.

estar pato: to be flat broke.

factura: a receipt for business purposes that allows you to recover the Value Added Tax (IVA) paid on any purchase.

Gabriela: a 5 thousand *peso* bill, named for Gabriela Mistral, the person on the bill.

gamba: a 100 *peso* coin or 100 thousand Chilean *pesos*.

Isapre: stands for *Instituciones de Salud Previsional*, and refers to any of numerous private health care plans.

luca: a thousand *pesos*.

mojar: to bribe, grease the palm.

MONEY, MONEY, MONEY, MOOOOO-NEY, *continued*

palo: a million Chilean *pesos*.

palo verde: a million dollars.

plata: moola, cash, money, bucks.

quina: 500 Chilean *pesos*.

recortín: a secret payment, like a commission for making something happen.

UF: stands for *Unidad de Fomento* and is an index in Chilean *pesos* that is used to adjust for inflation for long term debts.

UTM: stands for *Unidad Tributario Mensual* and is an index in Chilean *pesos* that is used to adjust for inflation for tax reasons and penalties.

vale vista: a cashier's check assured by the bank, that cannot be canceled before you cash it, basically a bank issued check.

malteo: grab someone by his arms and legs and throw or swing him up and down in celebration. *En tu cumpleaños no te salvas del **malteo**.*

malulo/a: something malicious or not well-intentioned. *El niño es **malulo**, le pasa pegando al hermano menor.*

malva: just like marshmallow, but thicker, less spongy.

malvabisco: marshmallow.

★ 💣 **mamón:** 1) a mama's boy, spoiled. 2) a quiet person.

mañanera: sex in the morning. *A los hombres les gusta mucho una **mañanera** antes de empezar el día.*

mandar a la porra: to tell someone to get outa here, go away.

mandar a lavarse la raja: to get the hell out of here, to go away.

💣 **mandar cagadas:** to fuck up, screw something up royally.

mandarle a la punta del cerro: to tell someone off.

💣 **mandarlo a guardar:** 1) to have sex or screw someone. 2) to obliterate or cream someone in a competition, completely wipe them out.

★ **mandarse un condoro:** to screw up, make a mess of things. *Otra vez te **mandas-***

te un condoro *revisando las cuentas.*

mandonear: to boss around. *La Marta es súper buena para* ***mandonear*** *al marido.*

mangazo: a punch.

manilarga: a thief.

manito de gato: literally "a cat's hand", to touch up your makeup, in the bathroom for example, comes from the action a cat does with it's paw while cleaning itself.

manjar: a typical caramel type sweet that is used in candies, pastries and all types of desserts, known as *dulce de leche* in Argentina. *Los alfajores con mucho* ***manjar*** *son exquisitos.*

mano de guagua: stingy, tightfisted, as in a baby's hand.

mano de monja: literally "the hand of a nun", means that a person cooks well. *Te quedó súper rico el queque, tienes* ***mano de monja****.*

manos de hacha: someone that breaks whatever they touch or hold. *Todo lo rompe, no cuida nada, es* ***manos de hacha****.*

manos de mantequilla: butterfingers, literally "butter hands", refers to someone that has a hard time holding things, that always lets them slip out of their hands, for instance, a soccer goalie that lets the ball slide through his hands. *Cuando lava la loza todo se le cae, tiene* ***manos de mantequilla****.*

mañoso: finicky, picky.

manso: 1) extremely large amount, a lot of. 2) huge immense. *¿La viste? Tiene* ***manso*** *poto.*

mantecado: a butter cookie.

mantequillo/a: sickly. *Los hijos de la Montse salieron bien* ***mantequillos****, siempre están enfermos con algo.*

manuela palma: to masturbate.

marcar tarjeta: to report in to the girlfriend or wife, to let her know where you are, or to spend some time with her.

marcela: a beer.

margaritas: dimples. *Me encantan las* ***margaritas*** *que se le hacen a Francisco cuando sonríe.*

María tres cocos: tomboy.

💣 **maricón:** a fag, flamer, fudge packer.

mariconada: a betrayal. *Me hizo una tremenda **mariconada**, no me pagó lo que debía.*

💣 **maricueca:** a faggot, a homo, fudgepacker.

marrueco: pants zipper. *Revísate el **marrueco**, parece que lo tienes abierto.*

martes 13: literally Tuesday the 13th, the Chilean equivalent of Friday the 13th, the typical day of bad luck.

marucho: gay.

más apretada que tuerca de submarino: literally "tighter than a submarine nut", extremely cheap, a cheapskate.

más apretado que moño de vieja: literally "tighter than an old lady's hair bun", extremely cheap, a cheapskate.

más apretado que traje de torero: literally "tighter than a bullfighter's suit", a cheapskate, extremely cheap.

más arreglado que mesa de cumpleaños: literally "more organized than a birthday table", someone that is overdressed, too produced or fake looking.

más arrugada que carta de amante: literally "more wrinkled than a lover's letter", someone really old.

más asustado que pez para semana santa: literally "more scared than a fish for Easter", extremely scared.

más blanco que poto de monja: literally "whiter than a nun's butt", pale white.

• más blanco que poto de monja •

más botado que colilla de cigarro: literally "more thrown away than a cigarette butt", basically means to be ignored.

más buena que el pan con chancho: a hot, attractive, or tasty person of the opposite s

más cagado que palo de gallinero: literally "shittier than a chicken perch", broke, poor, bad off.

más caliente que asiento de taxista: literally "hotter than a taxi driver's cushion", extremely hot.

más caliente que tetera de campo: literally "hotter than a country tea kettle", extremely horny.

más callada que cajera de peaje: literally "quieter than a toll booth cashier", extremely quiet.

más colorado que cogote de ciclista: literally "redder than a bicyclist's neck", extremely red.

más corto que cuello de almeja: literally "shorter than a clam's neck", short on money, broke.

más corto que estornudo de gato: literally "shorter than a cat's sneeze", short on money, broke.

• más doblado que chino con visita •

más cosido que botón de oro: literally "more sewn than a gold button", means extremely drunk and is a play on words between *cosido*, or sewn and *cocido*, or drunk.

más doblado que boleto de micro: literally "more folded than a bus ticket", drunk, trashed.

más doblado que chino con visita: literally "more bent over than a chinaman with visitors", drunk, trashed.

más doblado que conejo de mago: literally "more folded than a magician's rabbit", extremely drunk or high.

más empolvado que ratón de molino: literally "dustier than a rat in a mill", extremely covered in dirt or dust.

más enredado que abrazo de pulpos: literally "more tangled than a octopus' hug", a confused, mixed-up situation.

más escondido que boleta de motel: literally "more hidden than a motel receipt", used to express that you haven't seen someone for a while, they've been hiding.

más fácil que tabla de uno: literally "easier than the multiplication tables for 1 (1 times 1, 1 times 2, etc)", an extremely easy task.

más falso que cachetada de payaso: literally "more false than a clown's slap", fake or false.

más fea que azafata del caleuche: literally "uglier than a stewardess from the Caleuche", refers to a legend of the ghost ship *Caleuche*, since the stewardess is a ghost she must be extremely ugly.

más feo que el diablo chupando limón: literally "uglier than the Devil sucking a lemon", really, really ugly.

más flaco que piojo de peluca: literally "thinner than a louse in a wig", extremely thin.

★ **más fome:** extremely boring, dull.

más fome que chupar un clavo: extremely boring, literally "more boring than sucking nails". *Es muy perno, **más fome que chupar un clavo.***

más frío que culo de foca: literally "colder than a seal's ass", extremely cold.

más guasquiado que león de circo: literally "more whipped than a circus lion", extremely drunk.

más helado que los cocos de Tarzán: literally "colder than Tarzan's balls", 1) to be extremely cold. 2) to be broke, penniless.

más inútil que cenicero de moto: literally "more useless than a motorcycle ashtray", extremely useless.

más ladrón que gato de campo: literally "more of a thief than a country cat", someone that steals everything possible.

más largo que bufanda de jirafa: literally "longer than a giraffe's scarf", extremely long.

más largo que crédito hipotecario: literally "longer than a mortgage", extremely long.

más lento que caracol reumático: literally "slower than a rheumatic snail", extremely slow.

más lento que un bolero: a slow, lazy person.

más manoseada que fierro de micro: literally "more grabbed than a support post in a bus", most often in reference to an easy woman that's had more hands on her than a post on a bus (to hold on to while you're on the bus).

más negro que piojo de minero: literally "blacker than a miner's louse", extremely black.

• más negro que piojo de minero •

más negro que tetera de campo: literally "blacker than a country teapot", extremely black.

más nerviosa que monja con atraso: literally "more

nervous than a late nun (in reference to her period)", extremely nervous.

• más peligroso que mono con navaja •

más nervioso que testigo falso: literally "more nervous than a false witness", extremely nervous.

★ **más o menos:** literally means "more or less" but is often used to avoid a direct response of no to someone. For example if you ask your son if he did his homework, and he answers *más o menos*, the real answer is no, he didn't do it.

más peligroso que mono con navaja: literally "more dangerous than a monkey with a razor blade".

más peligroso que peruano haciendo mapa: literally "more dangerous than a Peruvian making a map", extremely dangerous, it is in reference to the border disputes that Chile and Perú have had since the 1800s, after Chile won part of it's northern land from Peru in the War of the Pacific, from 1879 to 1883. This area is extremely rich in many minerals, so has brought a lot of wealth to Chile.

más perdido que el Teniente Bello: literally "more lost than Lieutenant Bello", means to be completely lost and refers specifically to an aviator that took off for a short trip but was never heard from again. Almost 100 years later the whereabouts of the plane wreckage or Lt. Bello's remains are still unknown. *No cachó nada, andaba* ***más perdido que el Teniente Bello****.*

más pesado que un chupete de fierro: literally "heavier than a baby's iron pacifier", annoying, bothersome.

más pesado que collar de melones: literally "heavier than a melon necklace", annoying, bothersome.

• más pesado que collar de melones •

más pesado que maletín de gasfiter: literally "heavier than a plumber's toolbox", annoying, bothersome.

más pesado que tanque a pedales: literally "heavier than a tank with pedals", refers to a person that is extremely annoying, or as said in Chile, *pesado*.

más pesado que volantín de cholguán: literally "heavier than a kite made from hardwood", refers to an extremely annoying person, or *pesado*.

más problemas que maletín de abogado: literally "more problems than a lawyer's suitcase", someone in a lot of trouble.

más puntual que novia fea: literally "more punctual than an ugly girlfriend", since the girlfriend is so ugly, she will always show up on time, to avoid anyone stealing her boyfriend, means extremely punctual.

💣 **más que la chucha:** a shitload of, too much of.

más que la cresta: a whole lot of, too much of.

más quebrado que galleta de soda: literally "more of a show off than a soda cracker", penniless, broke, poor.

más quieto que caballo de fotógrafo: literally "more motionless than a horse for photographs", this is generally a cardboard horse, that street photographers use for posing with small children, means extremely still.

más raro que culebra con orejas: literally "stranger than a snake with ears", a weird person.

más raro que serpiente sin cola: literally "stranger than a serpent with no tail", a weird person.

más rayado que escritorio de liceo: literally "more scratched than a school desk", means extremely crazy, using a play on words with *rayado* which means both scratched and nuts.

más rayado que puerta de perrera: literally "more scratched than a kennel door", means extremely crazy, using a play on words with *rayado* which means both scratched and nuts.

más rollos que frenada de cuncuna: literally "more rolls than a suddenly stopped caterpillar", a fat person with lots of rolls on their body.

más seco que escupo de momia: literally "drier than a mummy's spit", extremely dry or extremely thirsty.

más sudado que caballo de bandido mexicano: literally "sweatier than a Mexican bandit's horse", extremely sweaty.

más suelto que tapabarro de citroneta: literally "more open than mud flaps of a little Citroen car", extremely loose, in reference to clothing, for example.

más tieso que un chuzo: literally "more rigid than an iron stick", extremely rigid, especially in reference to someone dancing. A *chuzo* is an iron bar that is used to break up concrete or to dig up earth.

• más rollos que frenada de cuncuna •

> **FILLER PHRASES**
>
> *Sprinkle some of these words into your conversations, and you'll fit right in.*
>
> **ahí estamos**
>
> **capaz que**
>
> **cierto**
>
> **cual es la gracia**
>
> **da lo mismo**
>
> **eso no mas**
>
> **fíjate**
>
> **igual**
>
> **ná que ver**
>
> **¿No es cierto?**
>
> **no estoy ni ahí**
>
> **ponte tu**
>
> **quedó pá la cagá**
>
> **si, po**
>
> **super-poco**
>
> **¿Te fijas? or ¿Te fijai?**
>
> **¿Te imaginai?**
>
> **¿Te tinca?**

más tiritón que espejo de micro: literally "shakier than a bus mirror", refers to a nervous or scared person that is shaking.

más traspirado que caballo de feria: literally "more sweaty than a fair horse", really sweaty.

más traspirado que calcetín de cartero: literally "sweatier than a postman's sock", extremely sweaty.

más traspirado que testigo falso: literally "sweatier than a false witness", really sweaty.

más viejo que el hilo negro: literally "older than black thread", extremely old.

mascar lauchas: see *peor es mascar laucha.*

💣 **mata de huevas:** an annoying person, someone that you can't even put up with.

💣 **matar la gallina:** to screw, have sex.

matasanos: a quack, insulting term to describe a doctor, literally means "kills healthy people". *Esa clínica está llena de* ***matasanos****, no es confiable.*

mateo: a geek, studious person always with his nose in the books, a know-it-all.

matutear: to sell things illegally, generally at the office or among friends, without giving receipts, collecting sales tax, or declaring the earnings. *Se obtiene mucho dinero, si te dedicas a **matutear** en la oficina.*

maula: a trap, a swindle.

mauloso: a cheater.

mazamorra: crushed corn usually combined with beans.

me carga: I hate.

meado de gato: to have bad luck.

meado de perro: to have bad luck.

💣 **mear:** to piss.

mechero: someone who steals clothes in stores by wearing them beneath his own clothes. *Pillaron a dos **mecheros** en la tienda.*

mechonear: 1) to pull someone's hair. 2) a hazing for new college students.

mechoneo: hazing. *¡El **mechoneo** de la Univesidad Católica fue de miedo!*

medalla: a clothing stain from water or food.

media huevada: a big thing.

★ **medio/a:** word used to highlight how extreme something is, for example la *media nariz* would mean a huge nose, and *media cagada* would be a serious mess of a situation. *Jorge dejó la **media** cagada en la oficina ayer.*

medio cucarro: buzzed, a bit drunk.

medio rally: a long, out of the way trip. *Mamá, no voy al Alto, tendría que hacer **medio rally** para llegar.*

medio raro/a: iffy, questionable, something strange is going on.

mejorarse: to give birth.

menos ritmo que una gotera: literally "less rhythm than a drip", no rhythm whatsoever.

★ **menso:** dummy, doofus.

menta: a mint-flavored after dinner cordial, used to help with the digestion.

merme: silly, stupid.

mermelado: goofball, dummy, doofus.

merquén: a Mapuche spice used to give things a hot flavor to them, similar to chili powder.

meter la mula: to defraud.

meterle chala: to go quickly, move quickly. *Siempre voy tarde, le* ***meto chala*** *para tratar de llegar a la hora.*

meterse en las patas de los caballos: to get mixed up in problems.

meterse en un zapato de chino: to get mixed up in problems.

mi pierna: romantic partner.

mi tío/a: generic term to refer to a person without mentioning their name. *Cuando* ***mi tío*** *apareció, me puse muy nerviosa.*

michellin: rolls of fat on the stomach, love handles. *Con este vestido, los* ***michellin*** *se me notan más.*

★ **micro:** a bus.

★ **mil hojas:** a typical pastry dough used for different types of desserts.

mil más caro: a whole lot more expensive.

💣 **milico:** an insulting term used for military personnel.

mina: babe, chick.

mina taxi: term for a fake blond, named for taxis in Chile that are yellow on the roof (on top) and black on the bottom (think this one through, you'll figure out the connection).

mish: 1). look at you, aren't we a little full of ourselves. 2) expression used to communicate surprise for a comment that is made. *Gané la Polla anoche. ¡****Mish****, mira tú!*

mistela: a drink made with *aguardiente*, cinnamon, quince, orange peel and clove.

miti-miti: 50-50, split down the middle.

mitómano: a constant liar.

mocha: argument, fight. *Se armó la tremenda* ***mocha*** *a la salida del estadio ayer.*

moco en la frente: something easy to achieve, for example an assignment at work.

mocoso: snot-nosed kid.

[$] **mojar:** to bribe, grease the palm. *Tuvimos que* ***mojar*** *a los pacos, para que no nos pasaran el parte.*

mojigato: to play dumb, eventhough you actually are not.

molear: to go shopping. *La Ange insiste pero yo no tengo ganas de **molear**.*

momio: extreme right side of the political spectrum.

mongo/a: fool, dummy, slow. *Es muy **mongo**, siempre hace leseras.*

moño de vieja: a mess, a problem, all tangled up.

montgomery: a rain overcoat.

💣 **morder la almohada:** gay, queer, literally "bite the pillow".

morenaza: a hot brunette.

★ **morir:** to be amazed, to die for. *¡Te **morí** lo flaca que está la Andrea!*

morir en la rueda: to keep a secret. *No podemos decir nada, hay que **morir en la rueda.***

morir piola: to keep a secret.

morir pollo: to keep a secret.

★ **morirse:** used figuratively to mean to die from embarrassment. *Me **muero** si Miguel viene a hablar conmigo.*

morirse el ala: to smell bad.

★ **mortal:** amazing, the best, cool, sweet. *El vestido quedó **mortal**, se ve precioso.*

mosca: signed initials.

mosquetero: a window screen.

mostrar la hilacha: to reveal one's stripes or to show what you're really made of always in a negative sense, to show your true colors, coming across as low class, or uneducated.

mote con huesillo: a dessert made from pieces of wheat or hominy and dried peaches, served in a sweet liquid, also consumed as a thirst quencher on hot days.

★ **motel:** Motels are generally geared towards providing a location for sexual encounters by, for example, hiding the identity of visitors and designing rooms to include romantic amenities like whirlpools, vibrating beds and mirrors. They are sometimes available on an hourly basis.

moya: answer means "no clue" or no idea. *Parece que*

***moya** pagó la cuenta, yo no supe quién fue.*

mucho ruido, pocas nueces: much ado about nothing, all bark and no bite.

★ **muerte:** excellent, awesome. *Viña en verano es la **muerte** con tanta gente para huevear.*

mujeriego: a player, a guy that uses women for sex and has no problems with dumping them and moving on to the next, always has a lot of women.

mula: fake, false. *Juan Carlos es muy **mula**, siempre trata de cagarnos.*

multiplicarse por cero: to leave, disappear, scat, scram.

muñequear: to boss people around. *Sergio siempre trata de **muñequearme** con sus cuentos.*

N

★ **N:** see ene.

★ **nada que ver:** 1) you're way off, not even close, you're completely wrong. 2) to not have anything in common, to not be similar, to not be related to the topic.

★ **nana:** maid, household help.

nariz respingada: 1) a pointy nose. 2) snobby, stuck-up. 3) to think you're the shit.

ñato: 1) flat-nosed. 2) a random person.

natre: extremely bad. *Mi sobrino es más malo que el **natre**.*

★ **natural:** refers to drinks that are served at room temperature. *Señor, ¿le sirvo su jugo helado o **natural**?*

★ **navegado:** warm red wine prepared with sugar, spices (like cinnamon and cloves) and orange slices. *En invierno es delicioso tomarse un **navegado**.*

ñecle/a: weak, delicate, fragile.

negra: term of endearment for a woman, generally between two women.

💣 **nepe:** the inverse of *pene*, or penis.

ñeque: force, muscle.

💣 **ni cagando:** no fucking way.

ni chicha ni limonada: not one nor the either, undefined, in between, undecided.

ni muy muy, ni tan tan: middle of the road, not one extreme or the other.

ni pico idea: no freaking clue.

ni un brillo: nothing special, nothing worth mentioning.

💣 **nica / ni ca:** short for ni cagando. ***Ni ca**, me van a ver en el concierto de Luis Miguel.*

ningunear: to underestimate someone, to play down their worth.

★ **no cachar ni una:** to not understand absolutely anything, to be completely lost. *El gringo no entiende español, **no cacha ni una**.*

no cotizar: to not appreciate or like someone. *Juan Felipe estuvo detrás de la Pili varios meses, pero ella **nunca lo cotizó**.*

no da el cuero: to be too worn out for the next activity. *Estoy muy cansada, **no me da el cuero** para salir esta noche.*

★ **¿no es cierto?:** right?, correct?, isn't that so?

★ **no estar ni ahí:** couldn't care less about something, this phrase is often said by someone that is angry or upset and is somewhat ironic, since the person using the phrase does actually care about whatever is in discussion. ***No estoy ni ahí** con que ya tiene otra polola.*

no fue culo: not being able to do something.

no funcar: to not be related to, not apply, not be relevant. *Creo que esto **no va a funcar**, son cosas muy distintas.*

no haber pelado ni una papa: comment after looking at the time used to mean that it's late and you haven't accomplished anything in the day.

no hacerse el leso: to not play stupid. ***No te hagas el leso**, yo sé que me entendiste.*

no hay de que: no problem, don't worry about it, often in response to a "thank you".

no hay pan duro: don't bother me, go away, for example in response to someone knocking on the front door.

★ **no más:** go ahead, no problem, just the way it is. *Mándame el archivo **nomás**.*

no nos veamos la suerte entre gitanos: you can't talk, you're the same way.

no pasa naipe: don't worry, everything's cool, nothing's going to happen.

no pasarle nadie: extremely rude or arrogant and for that no one likes to have contact with the person.

no saber con qué chicha estar curándose: to not know the problem you're getting yourself into.

no saber para donde va la micro: to have no idea of what the others are talking about.

no salvar a nadie: to be worthless. *El profesor no sabe enseñar, **no salva a nadie.***

★ **no sé cuantito:** phrase used to continue a sentence when you cannot remember a person's name or the word for something. *El **no sé cuantito** de cuarto grado se llevó el libro que me prestaste.*

ñoba: the inverse of *baño*, or bathroom.

novio/a: in Chile this is specifically fianceé, whereas in most Spanish speaking countries it is boyfriend/girlfriend.

¡nos cacharon!: we got caught.

nuca de fierro: term describing the partner of a cheating significant other, that doesn't realize what the partner did.

ñurdo: someone not capable of doing something, clumsy, slow, dimwitted.

O

★ **o sea:** I mean.

¡ojo!: be careful, pay attention.

ojito de gato: marbles.

ojo al charqui: pay attention, watch after this.

olor a rodilla: to be dirty and stinky from not bathing, comes from smelling like feet and ass, since the knee (*rodilla*) is halfway between the two.

★ **once:** afternoon snack or tea time often a social gathering more so than a small meal.

★ **onda:** feeling in the air, vibe, surroundings, environment. *¿Qué **onda** el nuevo jefe?*

★ **ondulais:** term to describe young women from upper class neighborhoods that grew up with money, are snobby, have curly or wavy hair and are often focused on maintaining their appearance.

• ondulais •

operado de los nervios: extremely calm, for example, someone that hears extremely bad (or good) news and only says "Yeah, okay".

★ **ordinario:** 1) sleazy, low class. 2) tacky, in poor taste.

oso: word that someone says when they put their hand out to shake yours, and as you grab to shake their hand, they quickly pull their hand back, they'll say *Oooso*, as in Gotcha!

ostiones: scallops.

oyehey: excuse me, listen up.

P

pachotadas: insults, cuss words, expletives.

pac-man: gobble up food. *Me comí toda la torta, parecía **Pac-man** del hambre que tenía.*

💣 **paco:** an insulting term used for Carabineros, the Chilean national police.

pacotilla: poorly done, done quickly, carelessly.

TYPICAL CHILEAN DISHES / COMIDA TÍPICA CHILENA

Use this as a checklist of foods to try (except for guatitas, ¡guácala!)

al pil pil: a form of preparing seafood, potatoes or vegetables with a sauce made of garlic, butter and oil.

Barros Jarpa: a ham and melted cheese sandwich.

Barros Luco: a beef and melted cheese sandwich.

calzones rotos: a fried dough pastry.

chacarero: a typical sandwich made of beef slices, tomato, green beans and green hot peppers, most often with *pan frica*.

chancaca: a sweet sauce used on top of *sopaipillas*.

chaparrita: a hot dog with cheese wrapped in dough, like pigs in a blanket.

charquicán: a stew made from ground beef and different types of ground or finely chopped vegetables.

choripán: *chorizo* sausage and a piece of bread, often as an appetizer at barbecues.

chorrillana: a Chilean dish of french fries, beef, some type of meat, scrambled eggs and fried onions.

chupe: a thick, creamy stew most often made with seafood.

curanto: a typical seafood stew from the Chiloé region.

ensalada chilena: a salad of tomatoes, onion and cilantro.

guatitas: Chilean dish of sliced cow's stomach stewed and served with sauce.

humita: mashed corn, wrapped in a corn husk and cooked.

lomo a lo pobre: a dish of beef, fried onions, and french fries, with a fried egg on top.

mote con huesillo: a dessert made from pieces of wheat or hominy and dried peaches, served in a sweet liquid.

paila marina: a traditional Chilean seafood broth.

palta reina: appetizer or side dish of avocado stuffed with a mix of chopped chicken tuna or turkey and onion, mayonnaise and spices.

TYPICAL CHILEAN DISHES / COMIDA TÍPICA CHILENA, *continued*

pastel de choclo: a Chilean dish made with chicken and corn baked in a clay *greda* dish.

pebre: a condiment prepared with hot peppers, onion, cilantro, garlic, tomato, salt, oil, and lemon, chopped up finely, served with beef or *choripán*.

porotos granados: a Chilean bean stew, that includes squash and corn, as well as several spices.

sopaipilla: a small, flat, round fried dough.

sopaipilla pasada: *sopaipillas* with *chancaca* on top.

tomaticán: a stew made from tomato and corn, that also includes onion, and spices.

Padre Gatíca, predica y no practica: to not practice what you preach, to not do as you tell others to do.

pagapeo: someone that takes the blame for everything, that gets blamed for everything.

pagar el pato: to pay for someone else's screw-ups, to take the blame. *Felipe rompió el vidrio pero la Naty **pagó el pato.***

pagar el piso: the custom that when someone new starts at a company and receives their first check, they treat all their colleagues to something, for instance a lunch, a drink, etc.

pago de Chile: to respond poorly to someone that was nice to you.

paila marina: a traditional Chilean seafood broth.

pailón: a very tall person, a little slow in his movements. *Mi hijo es tremendo **pailón**, se ve enorme al lado de sus compañeros.*

💣 **paja:** 1) jerking off. 2) lazy. *Me dio **paja** salir, hace mucho calor.*

pájaro: distracted, scatter-brained, airhead, flighty.

*Siempre dejo las llaves en cualquier lugar, soy súper **pájaro**.*

pajarón/pajarona: clueless, lost, distracted, scatter-brained, airhead, flighty.

💣 **pajearse:** 1) to over think an idea. 2) to masturbate.

pajero/a: a lazy person, with no energy, never does anything.

palanquear: to bother, tease, bug.

palanqueo: messing or screwing around.

paleta: a good friend.

paletear: to do a favor.

pálida: queasy, about to vomit, most often induced by alcohol.

palito en el poto: ants in your pants, can't sit still.

[$] **palo:** a million Chilean *pesos*.

palo grueso: a person who has money.

[$] **palo verde:** a million dollars.

paloma: women in the South of Chile, generally dressed in white, on the side of the road, selling different types of sweets and pastries.

★ **palomitas:** popcorn.

★ **palta:** avocado, another Spanish word is *aguacate*.

palta reina: typical appetizer or side dish of avocado stuffed with a mix of chopped chicken, tuna or turkey and onion, mayonnaise and spices.

paltón: rich, loaded, has money.

pan amasado: a typical Chilean bread often baked in a brick oven.

pan batido: another name for *pan marraqueta* or *pan francés.*

pan comido: easy, piece of cake.

pan de molde: 1) loaf bread. 2) a type of truck shaped like a loaf of bread.

pan francés: another term for *pan marraqueta*.

pan frica: a round type of bread used, for example, for hamburger buns.

pan hallulla: a typical Chilean bread round-shaped and extremely flat.

pan marraqueta: a typical Chilean bread shaped pretty closely to butt-cheeks, which obviously creates a lot of jokes.

pancha: a flat rear-end.

pancho gancho: a term referring to the city Valparaíso.

pancora: sunburned. *Fui a la playa y quedé como **pancora**.*

panfilo: imbecile, fool, brute.

pantruca: pale, white-skinned, pallid. *Con el vestido blanco me veo peor, más **pantruca**.*

★ **papa:** 1) easy. *Es **papa** hacer aseo, me demoro poco.* 2) a hole in the socks. *Me puse estos calcetines y tenían **papas**.* 3) a baby, or child's warm milk bottle, often before going to bed or upon waking up.

papaya: easy, piece of cake.

pape: a slap. *Si no dejas de molestar te voy a dar un buen **pape**.*

💣 **papiche:** describes a person that has a jaw that sticks way out.

papurri: term of endearment used with a close friend.

paquete: a guy's package.

para callado: something secret.

para la casa: split, get outa her, scram.

para la corneta: to be down, in a bad way, not well. *La terapia de hoy me dejó **para la corneta**.*

parar de gozar: Stop, it's too much!

parar el dedo: to not do anything. *Fui a puro **parar el dedo**, estaban en huelga.*

parche curita: a Band-Aid.

parqueado: alone and bored.

parte: 1) any type of transit ticket. *Viramos mal y nos pasaron un **parte**.* 2) a wedding invitation.

partner: a close friend, buddy, pal.

💣 **partuza:** an orgy.

pasado a revoluciones: an over-energetic person, wound up.

pasar corbata: to get by without problems, to slide through.

pasar en banda: 1) pass right through. 2) to be out all night.

pasar la vieja: to lose the opportunity for something.

pasar piola: to slide through, no questions asked.

pasarlo bomba: to have a great time, enjoy something immensely.

pasarlo chancho: to have a great time, enjoy something immensely.

pasarlo regio: to have a good time.

pasarse películas: to imagine the worst or to imagine excessively about something that hardly happens.

pasarse películas con alguien: to get the wrong idea about having a romantic relationship with someone. *Juan **se pasaba películas con** Claudia, pero ella realmente no estaba interesada.*

pasarse rollos: to imagine the worst.

pastel: 1) a loser, a worthless person, someone that doesn't work, but just sits around. *Los hombres con quien ella sale siempre terminan siendo **pasteles**.* 2) a bad surprise. *Estuvimos conversando y salió con el **pastel** que es casado.*

★ **pastel de choclo:** a typical Chilean dish made with chicken and corn baked in a clay *greda* dish and often topped with sugar.

pasto seco: someone who believes everything or is easy to convince of anything, gullible.

★ **pata:** foot.

pata de laucha: sick.

💣 **pata de vaca:** a shithead, son of a bitch, an extremely bad person. *No me quiere pagar mi dinero ese **paté vaca.***

patada en la guata: rude, not likeable, mean-spirited. *José es muy pesado, me cae como **patá en la guata**.*

patalear: to make a fuss, complain. *Si no nos dan aguinaldo, hay que **patalear**.*

patas negras: a person's lover, the other man or woman, in reference to when a person is married.

patatún: a sudden attack or health problem.

patatus: a sudden death.

patear: 1) to give someone the boot, the heave ho. 2) to push someone off, delay, for instance to keep rescheduling a meeting in an effort to avoid the person or situation.

patelaucha: sick, bad off, not healthy.

patero: a suck-up, a brown noser.

patiar la perra: to be angry and frustrated.

patiperro: a world traveler, someone that likes to keep moving, and not be in one place too long.

patita al hombro: sexual position where the woman is lying down on her back and puts her legs on the man's shoulders as he lays on top of her.

pato: broke, penniless. *No tengo ni uno para ir al cine, ando* ***pato****.*

pato malo: a bad person, a delinquent. *Un* ***pato malo*** *me robó en el Metro.*

Patronato: a sector of Santiago where there are numerous clothing stores, that offer extremely low prices. It is typical that some enterprising people buy clothing at these stores and then take the clothing to resell in their offices and to friends (*matutear*).

★ **patudo:** shameless, forward to the point of being insulting, or crossing an acceptable line. *Después de dejarme esperándolo todo el sábado ese* ***patudo*** *me pidió salir hoy.*

pavo: flighty, someone that doesn't think before saying or doing something. *Ese hijo mio es muy* ***pavo****; dejó las llaves dentro del auto.*

paya: a rhyming song whose words are most often improvised while the song is played/sung.

★ **pebre:** a condiment prepared with hot peppers, onion, cilantro, garlic, tomato, salt, oil, and lemon, chopped up finely, served with beef or *choripán*.

pechar: to freeload food, all for free.

pechoña: really religious.

pechugas: a woman's breasts.

pechugona: big-breasted.

pedir auspicio: to ask for money so you can go out on the town. *¡Mis hijos siempre*

DRUNK / COPETEADO

It's impressive how many ways there are to say drunk or hungover.

caerse al frasco: to drink too much for a long period of time.

chambreado: 1) buzzed, a bit drunk 2) something slightly warm, for example, wine.

chupar más que orilla de playa: literally "to drink more than a beach's edge", refers to someone that drinks extensively but is not necessarily drunk.

cocido: extremely drunk.

¿Cómo está el dragón?: how's the hangover?

componer la caña: to help recover from a hangover.

con los indios: hung over.

curadito: drunk.

curahuilla: drunk.

curarse: to get drunk.

dormir la mona: to sleep off a hangover.

el hachazo: hangover.

emparafinado: a bit drunk.

empinar el codo: to tip back the elbow, as in beer/ alcohol drinking.

entrar agua al bote: to get drunk.

estar cabezón: too much alcohol in a drink.

estar como piojo: to be extremely drunk or high, wasted.

estar entre Tongoy y Los Vilos: halfway between drunk and sober, buzzed.

estar raja: trashed, wasted, shit-faced.

guasquiado: more than a little drunk.

hacer la previa: to have a couple drinks to get things going before heading out for the night.

hacerse bolsa: completely wiped out, completely dead, from being tired or alcohol.

medio cucarro: buzzed, a bit drunk.

pegarse un guascazo: to have a drink.

pencazo: to have an alcoholic drink.

ponerse cucarro: buzzed, a bit drunk.

quedar botado: to be shitty drunk.

DRUNK / COPETEADO, *continued*

quedar tirado: to be shitty drunk.

rayuela corta: to tip back the elbow, as in beer/alcohol drinking.

resaca: hangover.

tener Cecilia: to be thirsty.

me están ***pidiendo auspicio****, y son adultos!*

pedir peras al olmo: to ask for something impossible.

★ **pega:** 1) work, the daily grind. *Mañana, no quiero ir a la* ***pega****.* 2) things to do. *Hoy tengo mucha* ***pega*** *porque mi asistente está de vacaciones.*

★ **pegar:** to go well together, to match.

pegar en la pera: to freeload on a free meal, at the neighbors' for example. *Vamos a* ***pegar en la pera*** *con la familia Marambio.*

pegarle mil patadas en la raja: a lot better than, more than. *El Porsche de Julio le* ***pega mil patadas en la raja*** *al Fiat que tiene su señora.*

pegarse el cuevazo: to be really lucky. *Se ganó el kino, se* ***pegó el tremendo cuevazo.***

pegarse un atracón: a strong term for making out, screw around. *Salí del pub y me* ***pegué un atracón*** *con una mina que no conocia.*

💣 **pegarse un culión:** to fuck someone in a one night stand.

pegarse un guascazo: to have a drink.

💣 **pegarse un pisón:** a whole lot of screwing, sex.

pegote: clingy, in reference to a person that is always hanging on another, lovey-dovey.

peinar la muñeca: to not make any sense, to be nuts, to go crazy.

peineta: an attractive guy, that always gets girls. *Jaime es súper* ***peineta****, siempre se ve bien.*

pela cables: nuts, crazy.

pelada: 1) an easy woman. 2) someone that steals another woman's boyfriend.

★ **pelado:** 1) dear, honey, sweetie; an affectionate term used with a close friend, child or partner (husband, boyfriend). 2) bald. *El **pelado** nos espera en el pub a las 8.*

pelador: a gossip.

pelambre: gossip.

pelar: 1) to criticize someone when they are not there. *1) En la fiesta, no dejaron de **pelar**, se notó mucho.* 2) to steal. *Me da miedo que me puedan **pelar** el Ipod en la micro.*

pelar cables: to speak nonsense.

pelar el cable: to not make any sense, to be nuts.

pelar una papita: to work, do something productive. *No he hecho nada hoy, no he **pelado ni una papita**.*

pelayo: 1) a type of chewy candy, most often made with milk. 2) a bald person.

pellizcar la uva: to flirt with someone else's boyfriend/ girlfriend.

pelo choclo: a bad hair dye job, generally blond. *Pelo choclo* is literally "corn hair" and refers to the roughness of silk from an ear of corn.

• pelo choclo •

★ **pelolais:** term to describe young women from upper class neighborhoods that grew up with money, are snobby, generally blonde with straight hair, are often focused on maintaining their appearance and are stuck up.

• pelolais •

pelotas: a guy's balls.

pelotera: chaos.

pelucón: a lot of hair.

peludo: complicated, hard.

★ **penca:** bad, not cool. *Que **penca** tener que trabajar durante las vacaciones.*

pencazo: to have an alcoholic drink. *Fuimos al bar el viernes a pegarnos un **pencazo**.*

pendejo: 1) pubic hair. *No soporto que la tina quede con **pendejos** después que se baña mi hijo.* 2) a kid, most often an annoying kid. 3) an immature person.

pendex: someone immature, often younger than the speaker. *Ella es muy **pendex** para salir con él.*

penquearse: to scold or reprimand someone.

💣 **peo:** a fart.

peo en un canasto: not mean a thing, of no importance, something or someone that won't be around long, literally "a fart in a basket".

peor es mascar laucha: things could be worse, better this than the other options, just be happy with what you have, literally "worse is chewing on a small mouse". *Debes aceptar ese puesto, **peor es mascar lauchas**.*

perno: nerd, dumb, slow, opposite of *mateo*.

perro muerto: dine and dash, to skip out on a bill without paying, for example, at a restaurant.

perro nuevo: foolish, dummy.

perro, perrón: term of endearment used with a close friend.

perso: person with a great personality.

★ **pesado:** difficult, unpleasant, hard to deal with. *El no me cae bien, es muy **pesado**.*

pescada: a chick with a hot body, but has an ugly face, in English the word butterface is sometimes used (as in everything But Her Face).

★ 💣 **pescar:** 1) to pay attention to. *Le estaba hablando pero no me **pescó**.* 2) to flirt, to have a connection with.

petaca: a liquor flask.

petizo: petite.

petróleo: diesel.

💣 **peuco/a:** an easy person, sexually.

piano piano: slowly, carefully, well planned. *Con ese asunto hay que ir **piano piano**.*

picada: a cheap neighborhood restaurant where generally the food is good and cheap and the decorations are simple.

picado: vengeful or worked up when someone beats you at sports, or steals your girlfriend.

💣 **picado de la araña:** promiscuous, slutty.

picaflor: a player, someone that hops from woman to woman.

pícala: hurry up, let's go.

★ **picante:** 1) disgusting, low class, tacky. 2) dirty minded.

picar la guía: motivate someone to do something "go after that chick staring at you".

picarón: a flirtatious person.

picarse: to get pissed off, get mad.

★ **pichanga:** 1) a plate of stuff to munch on such as olives, hams, cold cuts, pickled vegetables, etc. 2) to play soccer with friends or anyone who does not play well at all, just for fun.

pichí: pee, piss.

pichí de cangúro: white wine with pineapple juice, literally "kangaroo piss".

pichicatear: 1) to fix something, to jury rig. 2) high, from drugs.

pichín: a bit, a tad.

pichintún: a little bit of something. *Al cola de mono se le pone un* ***pichintún*** *de vainilla.*

pichocha: cute, in reference to children.

💣 **pichula:** a word for dick, but more between cock and dick in terms of harshness.

pichuliarse: to scold.

pichuncho: an alcoholic drink with *pisco* and martini liquor.

💣 **pickle:** 1) different types of pickled vegetables, such as onions, cauliflower and carrots, not just the typical pickled cucumbers. 2) trashy, sleazy, vulgar.

💣 **pico:** 1) dick. 2) mouth. *Cierra el* ***pico*** *y quédate callado un rato.*

picoroco: a large barnacle that may be cooked and served; the meat is removed from the shell and eaten. It's not actually as gross as it sounds. Often, when this word is mentioned, people laugh and giggle, as the pronunciation is almost exactly like the words for "crazy dick", *pico loco.*

picota: gets angry quickly.

★ **picoteo:** appetizers, a plate of food to munch on.

pie de plomo: walk softly, walk on eggshells.

piérdeteuna: a person who likes to be in all the parties, meetings.

pieza: bedroom.

pifia: 1) a mistake, error, a fault. 2) a zit. *Comí tanto chocolate, que la cara me amaneció llena de* ***pifias****.*

pifiar: to boo someone, typically by whistling, which is a common form in Latin America of booing.

pifiarse: to miss, whiff, strike out.

pije: snobby, stuck-up, often used in reference to someone of a higher social class.

pila: a battery.

pilcha: worn out threads or clothes.

pilín: a boy's wee-wee.

★ **pillar:** to get caught (red-handed).

pillar chanchito: to be caught red-handed, caught in the act. *Se mandó el tremen-*

*do condoro, lo **pillé chanchito.***

★ **pillo:** 1) clever, quick, sly. 2) a thief.

★ **pilucho:** 1) naked. *Cuando era niña, Diana siempre le encantaba andar **pilucha**.* 2) a baby's one-piece jumper.

★ **pinchar:** 1) to call someone once so their phone rings, and then hang up. This is used to let them know you called, or are arriving somewhere, for example, but you don't have to pay for the call. *Claudia, te **pinchamos** cuando llegamos más cerca a tu casa.* 2) to hit on or flirt with.

piñén: scum or dirt on your body.*Los cabros chicos siempre tienen el cuello con **piñén**.*

pinganilla: low class.

pinguinos: term used to refer to students in high school, in reference to the uniform that looks like a penguin.

★ **pino:** the filling used in Chilean *empanadas* made from beef, onions and raisins as well as spices.

piño: name for a group.

pinochetista: a supporter of the former dictator and president Pinochet.

pinta: someone's look, how they're dressed, their appearance.

pinta monos: unorganized, a screwoff.

pintar el mono: to scold. *Me **pintaron el mono** después de llegar 5 minutos tarde al trabajo.*

piojo resuscitado: a person that tries to appear as someone they are not.

piola: 1) discreet, keep a low profile. 2) quiet, relaxed, low key.

pipeño: an alcoholic drink similar to wine generally only made during Chile's independence celebrations *(Fiestas Patrias).*

piquete: the name for a group of policemen, often together to quell a protest or riot.

piquito: a benign peck on the lips, not a real kiss. *Encuentro fomes los **piquitos** ya que son muy de niños.*

piruja: ordinary, low quality.

pirulín: a guy's wee-wee, word used with little children in reference to penis.

💣 **pisar:** to screw a chick, term used generally only between guys.

★ **piscola:** a mix of *pisco* and a cola soda.

pista: road lane, another Spanish word is *carril.*

pitearse: 1) to break or destroy. 2) to spend. *Me voy a **pitear** diez lucas en ese regalo.*

piti: to not be able to see, either far or near-sighted.

pitiar: 1) to honk a horn. 2) to smoke pot.

pitiarse: break something, make something so bad that you destroy it.

piticiego: a near-sighted person. *Tengo que ir al oculista, estoy bastante **piticiego**.*

pito: a joint.

pituco/a: an elegant, high class person. Calling someone *cuico* is more of an insult than *pituco*.

★ **pituto:** influence, contacts, a special connection of some kind that can be used to get special favors. *Para trabajar en Codelco se necesita un buen **pituto**.*

pizca: a little bit of something.

★ **plancha:** embarrassment. *Pasé tremenda **plancha** cuando me caí en la calle y se me vieron los calzones.*

plasta: a loser, a worthless person, someone that doesn't work, but just sits around.

[$] **plata:** moola, cash, money, bucks. *Acuérdate de llevar **plata** para comprar pan.*

platudo: rich person.

★**PLR:** stands for *patada en la raja*, and means a kick in the ass, the boot, the heave-ho. *Cencosud le dio **PLR** al gerente de finanzas.*

pluma parada: someone who has no problem in facing others, a little arrogant.

plumón: 1) a bed comforter. *Con el **plumón** no necesito más frazadas en mi cama.* 2) marker used for a wipe board. *Rayaron mi auto con un **plumón** negro.*

★ **po / poh:** this is a filler word that has no meaning.

pobre huevón: someone pathetic, sad.

pochito: be full, from food. *Comi mucho asi que quedé **pochito**.*

★ **pokemón:** the main group in the Urban Tribes concept, that refers to teenagers and young adults that dress in skater tennis shoes and pants about to fall off. The males usually have long hair and sideburns, and generally a lot of piercings. Reggaeton is their typical choice of music.

• pokemón •

polera: a t-shirt.

pollo: 1) foolish 2) gets sick a lot.

pollo al velador: to go to a motel.

★ **pololear:** to formally be boyfriend and girlfriend. *Natalia y Pato se pusieron a* ***pololear*** *por fin.*

★ **pololeo:** an official romantic relationship. *El* ***pololeo*** *de ellos no va a resultar porque no tienen nada en común.*

★ **pololo/a:** boyfriend/girlfriend, the more common Spanish word is *novio.*

pololy: nickname for boyfriend or girlfriend.

★ **poncear/ponciar:** This means to make out with several people in the same evening. The object of this is to only see how many people you can make out with, without necessarily including any other sexual activity.

ponche: any type of wine punch with fruit added.

ponchera: 1) punch bowl. 2) tummy, stomach. *Tengo una tremenda* ***ponchera****, sólo de tomar cerveza.*

poncho: a wool blanket used by *huasos* as a type of jacket.

poner chala: to step on the gas.

FRIENDS / AMIGOS

These words all mean close friend, pal, buddy or something similar:

bestia
bruja
buena perro
buena wacho
cabro / a
chanchito
chiquillo
compadre
compinche
coso
flaco
gancho
ganso
huevón
loquillo
master
negra
papurri
partner
perro
viejo
yunta
zorrón

poner el gorro: to cheat on someone.

poner los cuernos: to cheat on someone.

poner un tema: the conversation's over, we're finished.

ponerle: to exaggerate, overestimate.

ponerle bueno: to put some effort into.

ponerle color: to exaggerate something.

ponerle todo el corte: to do something perfectly, with class.

ponerle wendy: to put some effort into. *Ya, hay que terminar el jardín, hay que* ***ponerle wendy***.

ponerse cucarro: buzzed, a bit drunk.

ponerse las pilas: to get going, to put some effort into it.

ponerse los pantalones: step up to the plate, take control of the situation, be a man.

ponerse rojo: to blush from embarrassment or nervousness.

ponle patita: get moving, pass it along.

★ **ponte tu:** for example.

popera: a young, fashionable girl that dresses similar to Pop music icons such as Britney Spears, Gwen Stefani, etc.

popin: word used with little children in reference to their private parts.

popo: poop.

• popera •

★ **por fa:** short form of *por favor*, please.

★ **por fi:** short form of *por favor*, please.

💣 **por la chucha:** For Christ's sake!, Dammit!, What the hell!

★ **por si aca:** short form of *por si acaso*, means just in case.

por si las moscas: just in case.

★ **porfiado:** disobedient, poorly behaved, rebellious.

★ **poroto:** any type of bean, other common Spanish words are *frijol* and *habichuela*.

porotos granados: a typical Chilean bean stew, that includes squash and corn, as well as several spices.

★ **porquería:** crap, junk.

porro/a: a bad student who does not care about their jobs or homework and never studies for tests.

porteño: inhabitant of Valparaíso. *Alfredo es una típico **porteño**, ama su ciudad.*

posta: a public health center, often used for emergency situations, generally smaller than a hospital, more along the lines of a public urgent care center.

potable: nice, good-looking. *Sebastián está **potable**, me gusta mucho.*

★ **poto/potito:** rear-end, heinie.

precioso: to be in jail. *Lo pillaron los pacos, está **precioso**.*

prendido: on fire, lots of energy.

prestar ropa: to defend someone no matter what he has done.

prieta: blood sausage, a more common Spanish word is *morcilla*.

principio de autopsia: one foot in the grave, about to kick the bucket.

★ **pucha:** shucks, darn. ***Pucha**, que fome que no resultó el viaje.*

💣 **pucheca:** tits.

★ **pucho:** a cigarette.

puente cortado: disagreeable person.

pulento: cool, awesome, sweet.

pulmones virgenes: literally "virgin lungs", refers to someone that's never worked before.

pun: a fart.

puñete: a punch.

punga: sleazy, disgusting, low class.

puro filete: a hot woman, great body and beautiful.

💣 **puta:** 1) Shit! 2) slut, bitch whore.

★ 💣 **puta la huevada:** shit, son of a bitch, motherfucker, an all inclusive statement after something bad occurs.

putazo: handsome man who can have any woman he wants.

💣 **puteada:** a tongue lashing with derogatory terms, cussing someone out.

💣 **putear:** to cuss out, bitch out, tell off.

Q

★ **qué chori:** how cute!, how cool!

★ **¿qué huevada?:** What the hell?

qué lata: 1) how boring! 2) what a pity, what a shame.

★ **¿qué onda?:** What's going on?, What's happening?

que saltó lejo el maní: to interrupt or enter into a conversation without being invited.

¿qué se teje?: What's happenin'?, What's new?

que top: sweet, cool. ***Que top*** *el auto de Paulina, es hermoso, último modelo.*

quebrado: a show-off. *Juan es tan* ***quebrado*** *que fue a la piscina en zunga.*

quebrarse: to feel prettier than everyone, proud of his/her look. *¿Por qué a los cuicos les gusta tanto* ***quebrarse****?*

quedado: a person that just sits around, doesn't do anything, instead of working to get what he wants.

quedar botado: to be shitty drunk.

quedar como chaleco de mono: to come across as bad, not impressive. *Habló pestes de mí,* ***quedé como chaleco de mono.***

💣 **quedar la cagada / quedarse para la cagada:** to be a messed up or fucked up situation.

★ **quedar la embarrada:** to be a messed up situation, a big ol' mess.

quedar llorando: to be frustrated.

quedar marcando ocupado: to be surprised by.

quedar tirado: to be shitty drunk.

quedarse con los crespos hechos: to be stood up. *Me arreglé para salir, lo esperé toda la tarde y no apareció;* ***¡me dejó con los crespos hechos!***

quedarse en la muela: to still be hungry after eating.

quedarse grande: to not be up to the task. *Al jefe le* ***quedó grande*** *el puesto de encargado de Perú.*

quedarse plop: surprised, caught off guard.

quemarse las pestañas: to work a whole lot, to work your ass off.

queque: rear-end.

quesillo: a light, white cheese often served with salads or as part of *once*.

queso: worthless or bad, generally in reference to a person's sports playing ability. *Ahí está el* ***queso****, ahí hay que pegar.*

¿Quién te metió ficha?: Who invited you?

quiltro: a mutt. *El perro de la mami es un* ***quiltro*** *muy bonito.*

[$] **quina:** 500 Chilean *pesos.*

quincho: an area in apartment complexes or houses that is used for barbecues.

quitarle el poto a la jeringa: to back off from something you said you would do at first.

R

★ **raja:** 1) dead tired. *Después de terapia quedé* ***raja****.* 2) ass. 3) drunk, trashed. 4) luck.

rajado: generous. *José me compró la cartera que me gustaba, es súper* ***rajado****.*

rajarse: when you pay something for the group, could be a party, drinks.

rajazo: tremendous luck.

rajudo: lucky, fortunate.

rajuela: a person with luck.

ramada: often the same as a *fonda* but may have a more permanent structure, such as a roof, whereas *fondas* are built up and taken down after every *Fiestas Patrias*.

rana: a mistake, screw up.

ranazo: pretend that you know about something, but really have no idea.

rancio: disgusting, disagreeable.

★ **rasca:** 1) poor quality, trashy, sloppy, tacky. 2) a sleazy, trashy person. *2) La gente que hay en la plaza es muy* ***rasca****.*

raspar: to get out of here, split. *Hay que* ***raspar*** *de aquí o nos van a pillar.*

rati: detective. *Los* ***ratis*** *buscan a un delincuente súper peligroso.*

• rayarse la pintura •

Ratón Pérez: the Tooth Fairy.

raya en el agua: not mean a thing, of no importance.

rayado: nuts, crazy.

rayar la papa: to be nuts, to be talking crap, not saying anything that makes sense.

rayarse la pintura: to rub up against someone in a sexual sense.

rayuela corta: to tip back the elbow, as in beer/alcohol drinking.

★ **-re:** prefix used to highlight the word it goes with, adds emphasis to the word.

★ **recado:** a message.

reclamar por el dedo chico: to complain about everything

[$] **recortín:** a secret payment, like a commission for making something happen. *De lo que me dieron para las compras me va a quedar un **recortín**.*

★ [$] **Redbanc:** the name of the ATM system, generically used to refer to any ATM machine. *Tengo que pasar* *al **Redbanc** para sacar plata antes de comer.*

★ **regalón:** 1) teacher's pet. 2) someone that you spoil.

regalonear: to spoil, to coddle.

★ **regio/a:** 1) attractive, hot. 2) well-suited.

relajante: really sweet tasting. *El postre estaba muy dulce, súper **relajante**.*

relajar la vena: to calm down, to relax.

★ **remedio:** medicine, other Spanish words are *medicina* or *medicamento*.

★ **resaca:** hangover.

resbalín de piojos: bald.

resentido: a person not happy with his own life and because of this criticizes others' lives, usually because of envy.

respingona: 1) a pointy nose. 2) snobby, stuck-up. 3) to think you're the shit, *respingona* is more insulting than *nariz respingada*.

★ **retar:** to scold. *Paula tuvo que **retar** a su clase completa, porque estaban hablando mucho.*

reventado: see *estar reventado.*

reventar: to go all out until not being able to do any more (at work, partying, etc.)

★ **rico:** 1) tasty, yummy, good. 2) hot, attractive, nice looking.

riña: a fight or argument.

rollo: a problem, a mess, a situation. *Me armó un **rollo** cuando mi esposa me vio borracho.*

romadizo: stuffed up, with a cold. *Me siento mal, amanecí con **romadizo**.*

romperraja: without thinking, impulsively. *Y salté del balcón de **romperraja** y por suerte no caí.*

ronaldo: word to refer to rum, or *ron* in Spanish.

roncola: a combination of the words *ron* and cola to refer to a rum and coke.

roñoso: dirty, poor.

ropa tendida: stop saying anything, used to let someone know that someone else is listening but you don't want to them to hear the conversation.

rosca: a fight. *Se armó la tremenda **rosca** a la salida del estadio.*

rosquero: person who likes to fight.

roteque: impolite, rude, cross the line of acceptable behavior.

★ **roto:** improper, out of place.

roto con plata: low-class, sleazy person, but with money. *Desde que gana más se convirtió en un **roto con plata.***

S

sabérselo por libro: someone that has all the answers, from being intelligent, well versed or lots of experience.

sacar de quicio: up to here with someone, completely fed up.

★ **sacar el jugo:** to use something to the maximum possible, to use something fully, literally "to pull out the juice".

★ 💣 **sacar la chucha:** 1) to beat the shit out of someone. 2) to hurt yourself, by falling down, for example. 3) to overextend yourself working.

★ **sacar la cresta:** 1) to have a serious accident, to really hurt yourself. *Me **saqué la cresta** el otro día cuando anduve en bicicleta.* 2) to work your ass off. 3) to beat the hell out of.

sacar la media foto: to take a photo, catching someone in a bad or compromising situation. *Te **saqué la media foto**, no andabas con tu polola, era otra.*

★ **sacar la mugre:** 1) to beat up someone. *Si no te callas, te voy a **sacar la mugre**.* 2) to squeeze the juice out of, to get as much out of someone as possible.

sacar la vuelta: to screw off at work, not do anything at work.

sacar los choros del canasto: to instigate someone, to make someone lose his patience. *Me agota su actitud, logra súper fácil **sacarme los choros del canasto.***

sacar pica: to provoke envy or jealousy. *Ya sé que tu vestido es mejor, te encanta **sacarme pica.***

sacar un siete: to get a perfect score in school, based on the 1 to 7 grading system used at schools and universities in Chile. *Amelia* ***sacó un siete*** *en su primera prueba del año.*

sacarla barata: to get away cheap, to avoid serious consequences in what could have been bad or serious consequences, a car accident.

sacarse los pillos: to release someone from fault.

💣 **saco de huevas:** a dumb, useless, foolish person.

★ **¡Sale!:** Oh, come on!, No way!, You're full of it!

salida de cancha: sweatpants.

salir canas verdes: to cause trouble. *Son tan porfiados que me van a* ***salir canas verdes.***

salir de parranda: to go out partying.

salir gente al camino: to have competition appear, for example, while looking for a job.

salir salado: to be extremely expensive. *¡Si va con toda la familia al cine, le* ***sale salado****, son 8 personas!*

salsa americana: although there are different variations of this common sauce, the closest comparison is relish.

salsa golf: a mix of ketchup and mayonnaise.

saltar la liebre: to have sex.

saltarín se llamaba el profeta: phrase used to indicate that you are there to ask the other person for money they owe. *Ya, ponte con parte de la cuenta,* ***saltarín se llamaba el profeta.***

salto y peo: doing things with no results at all. *Nunca concreta nada, vive a* ***salto y peo.***

saltón: paranoid, over- worried. *Desde que me asaltaron que ando* ***saltón.***

saludar a la bandera: to do something without commitment, carelessly.

salvar: it works, it's good, acceptable.

salvoconducto: a permit issued by the municipality that authorizes you to move from one residence to another. Without this permit, it is possible that the local police will seize any items you are moving.

sandía cala: guaranteed, definite, no risk.

sandwich: see *hacer sandwich.*

sangre en el ojo: to be vengeful.

sanguchito de palta: someone who doesn't know how to keep a secret.

sapear: to eavesdrop. *Mi vecina siempre está* ***sapeando*** *las conversaciones que tenemos en el patio.*

💣 **sapo:** pussy.

saquero: describes a referee that makes a lot of bad calls against one team.

★ **schop:** a draft beer.

scotch: adhesive tape, scotch tape.

se te cayó el carné: funny phrase used to tease someone who gives up their age in a comment they make, for example "I listened to the Rolling Stones all the time in college". ***Se te cayó el carné*** *cuando dijiste que escuchabas a los Rolling Stones en el colegio.*

★ **seco:** to be an expert at or really good at something. *Patricio es* ***seco*** *para la matemática.*

[$] **sencillo:** change, either in bills or coins. *¿Tiene* ***sencillo*** *para un billete de 10 mil?*

sendo: large amount of, a lot of, huge.

señora: wife.

ser/estar seco para: to be good at something. *Matías* ***es seco para*** *el fútbol.*

ser bueno para la pestaña: to be always sleeping. *Ayer dormí todo el día, soy súper* ***buena para la pestaña****.*

ser cagado: miserly, stingy, cheap.

ser doble A: a heavy drinker, as in Alcoholics Anonymous (AA).

ser lo último: to be the best.

ser último: to be a horrible, mean person.

ser orilla de playa: refers to someone that drinks a lot, specifically alcoholic drinks.

ser poncia: to be someone that likes to *ponciar*, make out with several people in one evening.

ser terrible de: to be very, very something. *El* ***es terrible de*** *chascón.*

ser un siete: to be a good person.

si la cago me avisas: when you know for sure that you screwed up.

★ **sí poh:** a typical phrase to agree with something.

sicosiarse: to overthink a problem, to the point of being obsessed.

simpático/a: indirect way of saying that someone is ugly, similar to "has a great personality" in English. *La amiga que le presenté a Julio era muy **simpática**.*

sintética: flat-chested woman.

★ **sip:** short for *sí, poh.*

siutico: snobbish, stuck up.

slip: men's underwear, specifically briefs.

sobar el lomo: ass kisser.

sobrado: arrogant and pretentious.

sobrado de cariño: better than expected.

sociegarse: to stay calm.

soltar la pepa: to tell the truth.

soltar las trenzas: 1) to live it up, let your hair down. *Hoy voy a salir a bailar, se me van a **soltar las trenzas.*** 2) for a gay man to begin acting like a woman for the first time.

★ **sonar cebollita:** overly emotional, mushy, melodramatic. *Yo quise creer en él y confié en sus palabras (**suena medio cebollita**, pero asi fue).*

sopaipilla: a small, flat, round fried dough.

sopaipilla pasada: *sopaipillas* with *chancaca* on top.

sope de tanque: a person that no one wants to be around, disagreeable.

sopeado: sweaty.

sóplame este ojo: You're full of it, I don't believe you.

soplanuca: gay.

soplar: to tell a friend the correct answers on a test at school, but trying not to get caught.

★ **sostén:** a bra, other words used in Spanish are *corpiño* and *brassiere*.

sota: ten of something.

★ **soy:** although this is the conjugation of the verb *ser* to mean "I am" this usage actually means "you", for example *"Que soy tonto"* should mean that I am a fool, but in Chilean means "You're a fool". *¡Pucha, que **soy** porfiado!*

soy tu padre: phrase means that the person completely dominates the other, in a given topic.

subir al columpio: to screw around with, tease.

submarino: beer with mint liquor.

suche: insulting term for a helper or assistant.

sucucho: a local bar to hang out and drink.

★ **súper:** prefix used to highlight the word it goes with, adds emphasis to the word. *Estoy **súper** complicado hoy para salir.*

supermam: a guy that chooses to spend all his time with his mother or wife/girlfriend rather than being with his friends, a momma's boy. *Ese tipo es **supermam**, por eso no consigue polola.*

superman: joking reference using a play on words with *superman* and *supermandoneado* to refer to someone that is bossed around by his wife or girlfriend, *supermandoneado* means extremely bossed around.

T

taca-taca: fusball or foosball.

★ **taco:** 1) woman's heeled shoe. 2) a traffic jam. 3) a piece of scrap paper to take notes on, as in post-its. 4) a pool stick.

taco de goma: someone who does not like to talk, usually because he is shy. *Cuando estamos en un grupo, siempre es Mario el **taco de goma.***

taimarse: to throw a temper tantrum, especially for children.

★ **talla:** a joke, a gag, a teasing comment.

también es cueca: could be, why not?

★ **taquilla:** young looking, fashionable.

tarjeta BIP: a prepaid card used for transportation on the Metro and TransSantiago systems.

tarro: old, worn out, worthless. *Este computador es un **tarro**, se demora N en partir.*

tarro con piedras: a noisy person.

tata: affectionate term for grandfather or grandparents (tatas). *Mi **tata** es muy amoroso.*

tatequieto: a punch. *Ya, deja de molestar o te doy un **tatequieto**.*

tato: shoe. *Ponle los **tatos** al niño por fa.*

taza: toilet bowl.

te caché: I caught you.

★ **¿te fijas?:** Got it?, Ya know?

te la hicieron: they screwed you over.

★ **te pasaste:** to go beyond what's required, great job, you really went all out!

¿Te pican los dedos?: phrase used when someone is scratching their ass.

💣 **teca:** short for *te cagaron*, they screwed you.

techeca: inverse of *cachete*, in reference specifically to butt cheeks.

tela: a cool person, someone that people enjoy hanging around, a good person.

tellebi: inverse of *billete*.

tener arrastre: to be successful attracting members of the opposite sex.

tener cecilia: to be thirsty.

tener el diente largo: to be extremely hungry, famished. *No he comido en días, **tengo el diente largo**.*

tener los dedos crespos: to be useless, not do anything. *Hazlo tú, acaso **tienes los dedos crespos.***

tener más raja que alma: 1) to be really lucky. 2) to have a big ass.

tener pasta: to be good at something. *Jorge **tiene pasta** para la computación.*

tener patas: to dare to do everything, shameless.

tenerla de goma: to have someone you boss around, as a secretary or assistant.

tenerlo cortito: without much flexibility.

tercer tiempo: the third half, in sports, it's when you sit down and drink after the game, same as the 19th hole

APARTMENT TERMS / TÉRMINOS SOBRE DEPARTAMENTOS

A few terms to help around the house:

ampolleta: light bulb.

cama de dos plazas: a queen-sized bed.

cama de dos plazas y media: a king- sized bed.

cama de una plaza: a twin-sized bed.

cama de una plaza y media: a full- sized bed.

dividendo: a mortgage payment.

gastos comunes: condo fee, monthly maintenance expenses for an apartment.

llave: the water faucet.

loggia: a utility room in an apartment.

pieza: bedroom.

plumón: a bed comforter.

salvoconducto: a permit issued by the municipality that authorizes you to move from one residence to another.

taza: toilet bowl.

tina: bathtub.

toalla Nova: paper towels, name comes from the brand of paper towel but now used generically.

water: 1) the bathroom 2) toilet bowl.

in golf. *El **tercer tiempo** va a ser en el Geo pub.*

terciarse: to run into someone. *Cuidado con **terciarse** con los pesados otra vez.*

terno: a business suit.

terremoto: a drink made from white wine, ice cream and liquor.

terrible pollo: a person who never talks or expresses her opinion.

💣 **tetas:** tits, in other Spanish speaking countries this word is more common to say breasts, but in Chile it is a strong word to use, the more typical word in Chile for breasts is *pechugas*.

tete: 1) a baby pacifier. 2) a problem, a situation.

💣 **tetona:** big tits.

tillas: tennis shoes, short for *zapatillas*.

tina: bathtub.

★ **tincar:** to want something, to interest, to sound good. *¿Te **tinca** ir a Mendoza el próximo fin de semana?*

tincola: term for red wine with cola. *Me hace mal el **tincola**.*

tintolio: another term for red wine. *Me encanta el **tintolio**, es muy saludable.*

tipin: about, more or less, in reference to time. *Nos juntamos **tipin** 5:30 en el restorán.*

★ **tipo/a:** 1) guy, dude/gal. *Ese **tipo** me cae mal por algún motivo.* 2) about, right around, in reference to time. *Nos podemos encontrar **tipo** 6 o 7, frente el edificio.*

tiqui taca: good, correct, well done. *Quedaron súper bien las llaves, todo **tiqui taca**.*

tirar: make out with someone, *grado 2*. *Me encantaría **tirar** con Sebastián, es muy guapo.*

tirar el poto para las moras: to back out of, to cancel at the last minute.

tirar para colina: to back out of something, like a date or business commitment.

tirar para la cola: to back out of, to cancel at the last minute. *No lo vuelvo a invitar, sé que siempre va a **tirar pá la cola**.*

tirar un chancho: to belch. *Al terminar la cena, el niño se **tiró un chancho**.*

tirar un churro: to give someone a complement, a *piropo*.

tirar un pun: to pass gas.

tirarse: to go out on a limb to try something.

tirarse a la piscina: to dive head first into something (figuratively) without knowing what the outcome may be.

tirón de orejas: to scold someone. *A mi sobrina le llegó un **tirón de orejas** por portarse mal.*

toalla Nova: paper towels, name comes from the brand of paper towel but now used generically.

tocata: a musical event, a concert, but smaller. *El grupo de Daniel participa hoy en una **tocata**.*

tocomocho: a car, transport. *Necesito urgente un **tocomocho**, me carga andar en micro.*

💣 **todas las micros le sirven:** phrase used to say that someone is easy, that any sexual partner will do just fine.

💣 **tole-tole:** a big old fucking mess.

tomar caldo de cabeza: to overanalyze a situation.

tomar el pelo: to pull one over on, to trick.

tomatelo con andina: calm down.

tomatera: a party where everybody drinks a lot.

tomaticán: a stew made from tomato and corn, that also includes onion, and spices.

tongo: a trick, deception. *El matrimonio de Marlen Olivarí fue todo un* ***tongo****.*

tony: a clown. *Me gusta el* ***tony*** *Caluga, es muy divertido.*

★ **top:** the best of the best, créme de la créme. *Que* ***top*** *el nuevo restaurante en Borde Río.*

💣 **topar:** to have sex.

toperoles: a woman's nipples.

topísimo: fashionable, cool, hip, happening, awesome. *Me encantó el jeans que compraste; se ve* ***topísimo****.*

topón: a small car crash.

torpedo: a cheat sheet.

torreja: 1) a slice of something, for example lunchmeat or cheese. 2) sleazy, tacky, low life.

torroncha: 1) sleazy, low class. 2) tacky, in poor taste.

💣 **tortillera:** lesbo, muff muncher, dyke.

tóxico: toxic, meanspirited, bad person. *Es súper* ***tóxico*** *el hueón, siempre tiene malas intenciones.*

tragarse un tony: dying of laughter, literally "to swallow a clown".

★ **trago:** a drink, a cocktail.

trancar la pelota: to block things, put up obstacles. *Su pega es esa, vive para* ***trancar la pelota****.*

tranquilein John Wayne: calm way down.

tranquilo el perro: calm down, relax a minute.

trapicarse: to cough or have trouble breathing caused by choking because of something stuck in your throat.

• tragarse un tony•

traspapelarse: to become extremely confused.

traste: rear-end, bottom.

Trauco: a mythological animal in the Chiloé region of Chile blamed for impregnating young women. Any time the father is unknown, it's blamed on the *Trauco*. *En Chiloé hay muchos hijos del* ***Trauco****.*

trepadora: woman who uses her physical attributes to get things, for instance a better job.

trillado: so common.

trompa: mouth.

troncomóvil: car.

tropical: white wine with pineapple juice.

troyana: a prostitute, slut.

truculencia: a trick.

truculento: tricky.

tucada: a lot of. *Cuando cobre la herencia me voy a quedar con una tremenda* ***tucada****.*

tufo: a stink, an odor, a stench.

tula: penis, when discussing with children.

tulyluly: a brown-noser that makes friends with people that can get him/her into parties and other types of events.

tuna: a gun.

tunazo: gun shot. *Le dieron un* ***tunazo*** *a ese delincuente.*

turnio: cross-eyed.

turro: a lot of.

tururu, tururú: craziness, out of control.

tuto: 1) sleep. 2) a baby's security blanket.

tuto de canario: extremely thin legs. *Se ve mal que tiene **tutos de canario**.*

U

ubicarse: a scolding word used at someone to remind them that they are out of place with how they are acting or what they are saying. *Oye, **ubícate** Leo, no puedes hablar así en la oficina.*

[$] **UF:** stands for *Unidad de Fomento* and is an index in Chilean *pesos* that is used to adjust for inflation for long term debts, for example mortgages. The value changes on a daily basis. Many types of payments are quoted in UF instead of in *pesos*, so the lender avoids any losses from inflation.

último/a: the worst.

[$] **un Arturo/Arturito:** a 10 thousand *peso* bill, named for Arturo Prat, the person on the bill.

un bache: a puddle, a mess.

un cacho de: a bit of, a piece of.

un chiste: 1) a person that is professionally worthless, doesn't do anything. 2) a person that's a clown, that's always joking, lots of laughs.

un plomo: an annoying, unpleasant, bothersome person.

★ **un siete:** this phrase means to be something 100%, and comes from the Chilean grading system in schools, which has grades ranging from 1 to 7, with 7 being a perfect score.

[$] **una Gabriela:** a 5 thousand *peso* bill, named for Gabriela Mistral, the person on the bill.

una pila de: a pile of, a lot of.

una tracalá de huevones: a crowd of people.

Usach: nickname for the Universidad Santiago de Chile. *Loreto estudia ingeniería en la **Usach**.*

uslero: a rolling pin, another Spanish word is *rodillo*.

[$] **UTM:** stands for *Unidad Tributario Mensual* and is an index in Chilean *pesos* that is used to adjust for inflation for tax reasons and penalties. The value changes regularly based on inflation. Many types of tax related payments are quoted in UTM instead of in *pesos*, so the effect of inflation is removed from the value.

V

💣 **vaca:** an asshole. *Le pegó super fuerte y demás lo pateó, es un huevón **vaca**. No quiso ayudar en el evento, es súper **vaca**.*

vacunar: to abuse someone's trust, generally by stealing money.

vagoneta: extremely lazy, worthless, vagrant.

★ **vaina:** a typical Chilean drink made from wine, vermouth and egg.

[$] **vale vista:** a cashier's check assured by the bank, that cannot be canceled before you cash it, basically a bank issued check.

valer callampa: to be worthless.

★ **valer hongo:** to be worthless.

Valpo: nickname for the city Valparaíso.

vampiro de las viñas: someone that drinks a lot.

• vampiro de las viñas•

vedette: a stripper.

vejestorio: someone or something old, antique, out-of-date.

vejestud: old people that think they're young.

veleidoso: backstabber, traitor, mostly used in reference to a woman. *No me gusta su actitud, es muy **veleidoso**.*

venado: someone that cheats on their significant other. *Ni se entera que es un **venao**.*

venderla: to screw up badly.

venir puesto: to be drunk. *El jefe **vino puesto** al trabajo después de las Fiestas Patrias.*

ventilador: a fan.

ver burros verdes: to withstand a lot of pain.

ver debajo del agua: try to see a deeper meaning in a situation, often to the point that you look for meanings that aren't there. *Siempre estás pensando mal, te encanta **ver debajo del agua**.*

💣 **ver la luz:** to cum.

verdes: 1) slang for Chilean police, the *Carabineros*. *Si los **verdes** aparecen, estaremos en problemas.* 2) dollars.

vereda: sidewalk.

verijas: nuts, balls. *Mi profesor de ciencia vive rascándose las **verijas**.*

verle el ojo de la papa: to have sex.

vestón: a formal jacket, also a jacket used by students as part of their uniform. *Sin **vestón** no puedes asistir a esa reunión.*

vida del oso: lazy, relaxed. *Se acabaron las vacaciones, no podemos seguir dándonos la **vida del oso**.*

★ **Viejito Pascuero:** Santa Claus.

★ **viejo:** a friend, pal, buddy.

viejo lobo: someone with a lot of experience in life.

viejo zorro: a clever old guy.

★ **vienesa:** a hot dog.

vietnamita: a hooker, an easy woman.

vikingo: macho, manly.

vino navegado: heated red wine with sugar and orange rind, served hot.

vino, dijo y se fue: phrase used to describe a boss that's never around.

virarse: Get the hell out of here!, Leave!, Get out!, Scram! ***¡Viráte**, estoy cansado de ti!*

visagra: a nosy person always looking out the window to see what's happening in the neighborhood. *Mi vecino es **visagra**, siempre está pendiente de lo que pasa.*

★ **¿viste?:** see, I told you so.

vitrinear: 1) to window shop. 2) to check out members of the opposite sex, as in window shopping.

vituperio: a party.

💣 **viva Chile:** an orgasm. *Hace tiempo que no grito **Viva Chile**.*

vivaracho: someone that acts on impulse but it turns out well for him.

vivo/a: 1) astute, clever, bright. 2) a know-it-all, that actually does not everything.

volado: 1) high, from drugs. 2) spacey, out of it, distracted.

volando bajo: down, depressed.

volantín: a kite, a more common Spanish word is *cometa*, and depending on the country the words *barrilete*, *chiringa* and *papalote* are also used.

volantín de cuero: someone that never pays anything, extremely cheap.

volar la raja: 1) to blow someone away, as in sports. 2) to put out extra effort.

volteado: so drunk.

voy a chanchar: to eat like a pig.

vuelto para el norte: completely lost, or dizzy.

W

💣 **warrior:** an easy woman just looking to sleep around with guys, slutty.

water: 1) the bathroom. 2) toilet bowl.

weón: alternate spelling of *huevón*.

whiscacho: a whiskey.

winner: a successful person.

★ **wuákala:** yuck, gross, disgusting, alternate spelling is *guácala*.

Y

¿y a mí qué?: What's that have to do with me?, What do I care?

¿y a vos... quién te auspicia?: Where did you come from?, Who brought you here?

¿y bombale?: and you?

¿y boston?: and you?

¿y qué fue?: and what happened?

¿y qué huevada?: What the hell's going on?

¿y quién le dio maní al mono?: expression used when someone interrupts, uninvited into a conversation.

¿y tu mamá quería mellizos?: literally "and your mother wanted twins", means that you are so stupid, imagine two of you.

★ **ya poh:** 1) enough, stop it already, cut it out. 2) sure, yes, why not.

★ **yanqui:** term for someone from the USA.

yap: short for *ya poh*.

yapa: a small gift, something free.

yapla: the inverse of *playa*, or beach.

yaya: a boo boo, a cut.

yayita: a hot woman.

yegua: a hot babe or chick.

yeta: someone who brings bad luck.

yo-yo: someone that always talks about themselves, selfish, egotistical. *Eduardo es un **yo-yo**; siempre habla de lo inteligente que es, de lo que sabe, lo que tiene y lo que ha hecho.*

yunta: best friend, buddy.

Z

zampar: to stuff your face, eating quickly.

zancudo: a mosquito.

zapallo: 1) big-headed. 2) a big rear end. *2) Con el tremendo **zapallo** que tengo, no me entra ningún pantalón.*

zapatear en una sola fonda: to be faithful to your partner. *Se nota que ese tipo **zapatea en una sola fonda**.*

zapatilla de clavo: to leave at the exact minute, often for employees that leave right at the hour, they don't stay a minute longer than they have to. *Los lunes hay que salir **zapatilla de clavo**, es un día muy largo.*

zapla: inverse of *plaza*.

zapping: channel surfing.

zarpazo de puma: put on too much makeup.

★ **zeta:** see *estar zeta*.

zonbeca: the inverse of *cabezón*, or big-headed.

💣 **zorra:** 1) pussy. 2) slut.

zorrillo: a type of Chilean police vehicle that shoots out tear gas.

zorrón: dude, extremely close friend.

zunga: 1) a Speedo type men's bathing suit. 2) underwear briefs. *Se ve muy guapo con **zunga**.*

About the Author

Suffering a typical 9-5 existence, Jared's foray into lunch-hour Spanish shook up his mundane life. He quit his job, stopped by briefly to school, and then left his country...for 14 years. Early stumblings in real-world Spanish taught him that a *cola* isn't just a soft drink, *bicho* doesn't always mean a bug, and *boludo* may be heartfelt or middle-finger felt. Nine countries, three business start-ups, two bestsellers and a Puerto Rican wife later, he is still confounded by how many Spanish words exist for *panties*. His quest is to discover all those words. In between, he meanders the Earth, dabbles in languages, drinks wine and sells shampoo.

Sufriendo la típica vida corporativa de 9am a 5pm, la incursión de Jared en el español durante sus horas de almuerzo le dieron el giro a su vida común. Dejó su empleo, realizó estudios y luego abandonó su país... por 14 años. Sus inicios con el español del mundo real le enseñaron que la *cola* no es sólo una bebida carbonatada, que *bicho* no siempre significa un insecto y que *boludo* puede tener una connotación cordial y también insultante. Después de una trayectoria de nueve países, tres empresas fundadas, dos libros en las listas de los más vendidos y una esposa puertorriqueña, Jared sigue confundido por la cantidad de palabras que existen en español para *panties*. Su meta es descubrir todas esas palabras. Mientras tanto, él pasea por el mundo, coquetea con los idiomas, bebe vino y vende champú.

Any comments, corrections or inclusions should be sent to
Pueden enviar cualquier comentario, corrección o sugerencia a
Jared@SpeakingLatino.com.

Other books from Jared Romey's Speaking Latino series

Speaking Boricua
A Guide to Spanish
from Puerto Rico

Speaking Phrases Boricua
A Collection of Wisdom and
Sayings from Puerto Rico

Speaking Argento
A Guide to Spanish from Argentina

Follow Speaking Latino and Jared Romey

Facebook Pages
Speaking Latino
Jared Romey

Twitter
@jaredromey

Google +
Speaking Latino

Speaking Latino Website & Blog
Search the FREE database with more than 8,000 slang words and phrases from Latin America at www.SpeakingLatino.com

CPSIA information can be obtained at www.ICGtesting.com
Printed in the USA
LVOW11s0241300715

448193LV00020B/192/P